Retreats to Go

Retreats to Go

Twelve Creative Programs that Renew and Refresh

Susan J. Foster

Foreword by
Maren C. Tirabassi

WIPF & STOCK · Eugene, Oregon

RETREATS TO GO
Twelve Creative Programs that Renew and Refresh

Wipf & Stock
An Imprint of Wipf and Stock Publishers
199 W. 8th Ave., Suite 3
Eugene, OR 97401

www.wipfandstock.com

PAPERBACK ISBN: 978-1-5326-4456-6
HARDCOVER ISBN: 978-1-5326-4457-3
EBOOK ISBN: 978-1-5326-4458-0

Manufactured in the U.S.A.

With loving thanks to Anne and Pete Foster for making me go to
Sunday School, but more importantly, for modeling the love of God.
Thank you.

Jesus said, "Come away to a deserted place all by yourselves and rest a while." For many were coming and going, and they had no leisure even to eat. And they went away in the boat to a deserted place by themselves.

– MARK 6:31–32

Contents

Foreword

Maren C. Tirabassi

I have been stressed by work and retirement, by family issues and self-doubts. I have been lonely and wanted a new community, and I also have realized that my engagement with a particular community is extensive but superficial. I have been vulnerable from losses of many different kinds, I have experienced grief, and I have brinked on new decisions, seeking guidance.

I know what it is to need a retreat.

I've been blessed and nurtured by a wonderful retreat. I've also been exposed to a dreadful one and counted the hours till the final *agape* meal. I hope I've never led that retreat, but I suspect that, carelessly assuming goodwill, prayer, and beautiful scenery were enough, I probably have. Creating the content, style, and atmosphere of a retreat experience is a delicate and important ministry.

Sue Foster is making this good work a lot easier. Her resource is a gift to planners of retreats and other shorter programs. She brings to it the authenticity of her thirty years of ministry and her ongoing intentional use of the retreat format to nurture congregations. She has personally led every one of the retreats included in this book, rather than merely dreaming them up, so she offers us readers the benefit of her planning as well as the wisdom of post-retreat evaluation.

There are some very specific gifts.

Sue gives detailed content in a mix-and-match layout so that a retreat planner can use each of the twelve themes at any different length. She also provides general guidelines and specific advice on the retreat format itself so that a reader can choose a completely different theme or scripture and create unique content following her pattern.

Sue also understands long ministry in one congregation, and addresses the need of former participants for an experience to be "just as good as last year," and the need of newcomers to be immediately included so they do not feel like outsiders.

Sue creates an environment that is safe for introverts, fun for extroverts, and compassionate for all. By encouraging a team process for retreat planning, she also leaves a blessing possibility open. Even while being responsible for leadership and the caretaking of participants, the pastor, lay leader, or faith formation director who coordinates the event also can be renewed and refreshed. We all know what it is to need a retreat!

Acknowledgments

MANY PEOPLE HELPED BRING this labor of love to life. I am deeply grateful for their help and support.

Heartfelt thanks to:

- Rev. Maren Tirabassi, book coach and wise mentor. This book wouldn't exist without your help and encouragement.

- Early readers of my manuscript: Rev. Oscar Brockmeyer, Rev. Mary Anne Dorner, Rev. Jane Hale, Rev. Sara Jane Munshower, Karen Ziehl who told me not to give up.

- Patti Burkett for traveling hundreds of miles to provide thoughtful suggestions, patient proof-reading, and lifelong friendship.

- Rev. Dr. Meredith Jeffers for long lunches filled with creative suggestions and enthusiasm.

- Amy Kinney, art therapist and creative person extraordinaire, for many delightful craft ideas.

- My personal IT team: Glen Lessig, Jeff Wong, and especially Ben Gould for infinite patience while leading me through the intricacies of formatting.

- Kevin Rainwater for fabulous, creative song suggestions.

- "Field Testers": Dawn Adiletta, Nancy Blodgett, Barbara Bocchino, Dotty Butler, Marie Chamberlin, John Davis, Jude Dion, Yvonne Dion, Kerstin Forrester, Nancy Gale, Ben Gould, Lisa Hibbard, Dot Hill, Amy Hiller-White, Sherri Kristal, Valerie Law, Dawn Morin, Ethel O'Keefe, Jill Relahan, Joyce Rivers, Dorrie Scranton, Roger Solomon, Anne Sorensen, Heidi Tucker, Jeanette Werstler, Nancy Young.

Rev Carly Stucklen and the congregation of the First Congregational Church of LaGrange IL.

- The entire congregation of the East Woodstock Congregational (UCC) Church for sharing three decades of ministry as we discover together what it means to serve God as the Body of Christ.

- Mike Foster & Jill Jensen, Dave Foster & Marianne Jorgensen for opening their lovely homes to provide a "retreat-like" atmosphere for writing inspiration.

- Dan, Rachel, and Jacob for providing good humor, creative ideas, and a reliable cheering section.

- Roger, for everything.

Introduction, or
"So, you want to go on retreat!"

Jesus said, "Come with me by yourselves to a quiet place and get some rest." (Mark 6:31, NIV)

Who is this book for?

IT'S FOR YOU! WHETHER you are an experienced retreat leader or considering your first attempt, this helpful guide offers creative ideas for themes, discussion questions, music, worship, and crafts. This book is for busy pastors, priests, Christian educators, youth leaders, fellowship groups, and anyone who would like to lead a time of retreat but may not have the resources or time to plan. Each retreat includes scriptural context, discussion questions, worship materials, and suggestions for music, images, and activities to encourage spiritual growth and conversation.

The flexible format can be used in a single gathering, a series of short programs, or a twenty-four- or forty-eight-hour retreat.

What is a retreat?

A retreat can be any time intentionally set aside for fellowship, learning, worship, and renewal. The most important elements of a retreat are the ones named by Jesus:

- An opportunity to *come away* from our usual routine.
- Some *quiet time* without the usual interruptions of computers, calendars, phones, and responsibilities.

- An opportunity to *rest*—to pause, at least momentarily, from worries, schedules, and burdens.

Any time away or any change in routine can be a breath of fresh air in a crowded calendar. A retreat might be:

- A Saturday morning at your church or another location
- A weekday evening or a series of evenings with a theme
- All day Saturday
- A federal holiday like Veteran's Day or Martin Luther King Day
- A twenty-four-hour experience at a camp or retreat center
- A full weekend away.

What are some benefits of a retreat?

A retreat provides a relaxed, gentle atmosphere where participants can engage in meaningful conversation while being spiritually fed and nurtured. A retreat is not an escape, but rather a time of rejuvenation and an opportunity to ground ourselves in God's steadfast peace and new life.

Retreats have the power to break through the isolation and loneliness that are often part of modern life. A retreat can feed our parched souls, soothe our harried minds, and quiet society's endless noise so we can hear God's loving voice.

The benefits of retreat time are far-reaching. Not only do participants return with renewed spirits, they can share their enthusiasm, insights, and learnings with the entire congregation. New or renewed friendships can spread a joyful sense of fellowship to the entire faith community.

As a bonus, retreat leadership can be fun, as well as personally and spiritually rewarding. It is an opportunity for the leader to learn and grow while offering participants a deeper understanding of themselves and their relationship with God.

Where can a retreat happen?

Almost anywhere! Going on a retreat doesn't have to be expensive or require a lot of traveling. The only real requirements are comfortable seating for everyone and a space that is warm/cool enough for comfort.

Take some time to find a comfortable setting for your retreat. Few settings are "perfect," but all have positive components that help set the attendees at ease.

Here are some things to look for:

- A gathering room where everyone can fit comfortably in one circle (no inner/outer circles).

- It is helpful but not essential to have space for breakout groups. If a large group breaks into smaller discussion groups, it aids conversation for each group to have a quiet place to meet and talk.

- Comfortable sleeping quarters (if staying overnight). Most people prefer not to have bunk beds or share space with multiple roommates. Generally speaking, the smaller number of people sharing a room, the more comfortable participants will be.

- Meals provided. Some will disagree, since cooking together can be a bonding experience, but for most people it is a real treat not to have to worry about planning, cooking, and cleaning up after a meal. Even the simplest meal (we often order a deli plate, chips, and drinks) can feel luxurious when someone else prepares it.

How can people be encouraged to experience a retreat?

As retreat leaders, your task is to invite people to discover the value of retreat time. There can be resistance or hesitation as people wonder whether they can set aside a few hours, maybe even a couple of days, to tend to their spirits, nurture their souls, or listen for that still, small voice of God. It can be an overwhelming challenge for some to carve time into an already overfilled calendar for something that may initially appear to be a luxury or a frivolous use of valuable time.

The first challenge for a retreat leader is to describe the importance of making time for spiritual renewal.

Use a variety of methods to advertise the retreat well. The church website, worship bulletin, social media, and even a bulletin board can be valuable tools. Word of mouth and personal invitations will encourage those who may never have attended a retreat before.

Scholarships that cover the fee partially or entirely will enable more people to attend. Some churches offer participants the voluntary option of making a donation toward the cost of another person attending; this can help establish a scholarship fund for those who are financially challenged.

Child care can be an issue for many. A youth group or a local Scout, 4-H, or other service group may be willing to help in order to allow busy parents to enjoy some time away.

When is the right time for a retreat?

Right now! Jesus was a busy person. He had much on his mind. And yet, repeatedly he urged his disciples to "come away" to a quiet place to pray, listen for God's voice, relax, share a meal, and be renewed. In doing so, Jesus invited his disciples to discover the creative movement of God's Holy Spirit.

Jesus never said, "Come away when . . ."

- Your work is complete
- Your worries are over
- All the hungry are fed
- The poor have received relief
- You have your life together
- You have extra time
- It's easy

Jesus made time to slip away into the wilderness for prayer and renewal. We need to do the same. As retreat leaders, our job is to reassure participants that they are worth the time and effort it takes to enjoy a retreat. We can help people understand that a retreat is a gift to themselves. Participants can enjoy reflection, fellowship, and laughter while receiving food for thought and sustenance for their spirits.

Is a retreat a one-person job?

No! Form a retreat team!

Maybe crafts aren't your thing. Perhaps leading music makes you uneasy. Maybe you're more of an idea person than a "stand up and talk to a crowd" person. Or you just don't have time to take on one more task. Ask for help! Don't think that you must do all the planning and preparation on your own. Engaging volunteers will help you and add another layer of creativity and energy to the retreat itself. Form a team of two to four people to brainstorm and dream about the possibilities for your retreat. Listen to their good ideas and enlist their help before and during the retreat.

Once you have settled on your retreat date and theme, start inviting people to share their gifts. People are glad to offer their interests and hobbies. Some retreats I have led were enriched by:

- A person who loves yoga sharing an easy routine.
- A poet leading simple creative writing.
- An accomplished gardener leading a nature walk.
- A musician serenading us on her guitar.
- A community actor teaching theater games.
- A history buff bringing stories related to our theme.

Your participants can be a rich source of ideas and experiences. Invite them to bring a picture, poem, or quote that relates to the retreat theme. These moments of personal sharing can also provide a meaningful way for participants to deepen their understanding of one another.

How many people are needed for a successful retreat?

There's no magic number. I have led retreats with as many as thirty people and with as few as five. Each experience provides a rich opportunity for group bonding, thought-provoking conversations, much laughter, and cherished memories. Don't talk yourself out of a retreat simply because you don't have large numbers.

What's the first step?

Read this book! Take time to read several chapters and choose a theme that appeals to you and will spark the imagination of your participants. There is always an excuse not to go on retreat. Now is the time to say yes to the invitation to "come away" and immerse yourself in God's presence.

Chapter 1

Preparing for Your Retreat

EACH CHAPTER INCLUDES RESOURCES to streamline your planning as you create a retreat that will renew and refresh participants. You may want to read through several retreats before choosing which one to use first. Use the tools provided to plan and advertise your next retreat.

Title:

The descriptive title conveys the essence of the retreat's theme. Use this to advertise the retreat and invite people to join in.

About the Theme:

This description conveys the focus of the retreat and offers a synopsis of the topics covered. It can be used in advertising your retreat in newsletters, bulletins, and on your website and social media.

Scripture Focus:

The selected scriptures form the foundation of the theme, discussion questions, craft ideas, music, and worship materials. When multiple translations are suggested, a website like BibleGateway.com is helpful.

"Quotable":

The quotes in each chapter capture the spirit of the retreat and can provide a lasting reminder of the retreat experience; use these to advertise the retreat and in follow-up emails or reports at the retreat's conclusion.

Use the quotes often! Some ways to make them visible during the retreat include:

- Displaying them throughout your retreat space.
- Printing them on "table tents" on the dining tables.
- Including them in any printed material you hand out.
- Printing bookmarks for participants to take home.
- Including them in the follow-up email to participants following the retreat.

Icebreakers, Name Games, and Introductions:

Be sure to take time for these fun, simple exercises. Even if your group thinks they know one another, there are bound to be varying levels of friendships and rapport. These exercises encourage participants to relax, get acquainted, and laugh together as they begin to share bits of information about themselves.

A list of icebreakers and name games can be found in the Appendix.

Introductory Objects and Bring-Along Items:

Each chapter suggests a theme-related object for participants to bring as a way of introducing themselves and as a creative way to build your worship area. Be sure to communicate with participants so they can choose a symbol to show the group.

These symbols can be shared following a time of icebreakers and name games. Often these objects are very meaningful to the participants, so it is important to create a safe, respectful atmosphere in which everyone is comfortable talking about their symbol. Sufficient time should be allowed to encourage everyone to learn each other's names and to get to know something about one another before asking participants to reflect on the object they have brought along.

If the group is large, you may choose to have only part of the group share at any one time. Gauging your group size will allow you to suggest how long each person's object description should be so the group is still attentive for the last folks. Start with a person who you know is neither rambling nor too terse.

Prior to the retreat, you may also invite participants to think about songs, readings, images, or poems that relate to the retreat theme. Depending on how many people respond, these can be shared throughout your retreat time prior to group activities, before or during worship, and before or after craft time.

In addition, participants can provide a wealth of resources for crafts or other necessary supplies—don't be afraid to crowdsource!

Leader's Tip:

These handy tips offer reminders to help you prepare for your retreat.

Video and Graphic Resources:

Download or print out these resources prior to the retreat.

Music Resources:

Music is a rich component of any retreat. A diverse list of hymns and songs for each theme offers options for worship or group gatherings. Songs can also provide a transition when you are regathering after a break. Instead of diving right into the next activity, a song can be a powerful way to quiet down conversations and refocus the group.

Alternatively, you may choose one song as a recurring theme for your retreat and enjoy several versions. This allows participants to repeatedly hear the lyrics presented in a variety of ways.

You can download a collection of songs on a smartphone or computer so they will be easily accessible. Depending on the familiarity of the song, you may want to print or project the lyrics (if copyright restrictions allow) so people can follow along.

Additional song suggestions can be found in the Appendix.

Hymns:

Both the title and hymn tune are listed to aid in finding particular hymns. If your church has a copying license, you may have permission to copy and distribute lyrics. Many hymnals grant permission to reproduce hymns for one-time use in worship settings; be sure to include the proper acknowledgement. Alternatively, some retreat settings provide hymnals or songbooks; prior to the retreat, ask what is available.

Any hymn that in the public domain is noted in this book and may be freely reproduced. A comprehensive list of public domain hymns can be found online.

Songs:

Songs may be purchased from sites like iTunes or Google Play. This is a good option, particularly if your setting lacks internet access. Alternatively, thousands of songs can be found (often with lovely video accompaniment) on YouTube for free. If internet connection is not available at the retreat site, download them onto your computer beforehand.

Gathering Your Materials:

Compiling the necessary items for group gatherings and crafts is an essential part of retreat preparation.

It can be helpful to divide materials into separate bags so you have what you need immediately upon arrival (such as worship area supplies and name tags in one bag, items for crafts in another bag, and so on). If you do yourself the favor of organizing your supplies before you leave, your retreat will run more smoothly and you won't lose time searching for things.

You may decide to put together a retreat kit that holds often-used items such as pens, markers, masking tape, clear tape, name tags, candles, lighter or matches, and so on. This will provide the basics necessary for any retreat; additional items can be supplemented for a specific retreat theme.

Creating the Atmosphere—Preparing Your Retreat Space:

Create a warm, inviting atmosphere filled with visual cues about your retreat's theme by using the suggested quotes and visual materials. This is also the time to prepare your worship space and altar with the suggested symbols.

You can introduce a gently interactive activity by hanging up one to three "Question of the Day" posters that you have made ahead of time. Questions can be found in the Appendix. This can be a fun way for participants to share thoughts and reactions anonymously.

Worship Resources:

Worship is a vital component of a retreat which welcomes participants into God's presence to receive God's renewing word. The rich array of Scriptures, creative litanies, prayers, and music celebrate God's forgiveness, healing, and new life. Additional worship resources can be found in the Appendix.

The atmosphere during a retreat is, by definition, more relaxed than in a formal sanctuary setting; participants can engage in worship (as they are willing and able) by reading Scripture, leading songs, sharing a reading, or offering another gift or talent.

The retreat can begin with worship; additional brief "worship moments" can occur at the beginning or end (or both) of any group gathering. Whether your retreat lasts for days or hours, closing worship can offer participants an opportunity to review highlights of the retreat; this can be a rich time of sharing. You may choose to celebrate communion, or not, depending on your tradition and the needs of your group.

Do not underestimate the power of silence in worship. Silence is a rare commodity in our hyper-connected, noisy society; allow people the luxury of enjoying some moments of stillness following a reading or a song. This can be an opportunity for reflection, which permits meaningful words or lyrics to sink in. Often the best sermon is the unspoken one.

Creating an altar/worship space:

Many people are visual learners who will absorb more from a physical display than any written and spoken words. It is worth your time to create a worship area with simple visual cues as a reminder of God's presence, as well as the particular theme of that retreat. Each chapter includes a suggested list of symbols for the particular theme. A high stool, low coffee table, or tray table can be draped with a scarf or piece of fabric to clearly establish the worship center.

The worship space will grow and evolve over the course of your time together as participants add their own objects or items created during group gatherings.

Discussion Questions and Activities for Group Gatherings:

Time for reflection and an opportunity to share in small and large groups are key components of a retreat. Participants are invited to reflect on Scripture, music, and their life experience; many people appreciate time to consider the questions on their own before sharing with the group.

Small groups of three to six people ensure that every person has an opportunity to speak. When gathered with the large group, be mindful of time management and the importance of providing "air time" for everyone. As the leader, it is your responsibility to be aware of who might want to share, but hasn't yet had the opportunity.

Crafting Our Message:

These craft ideas allow participants to create a tangible reminder of the retreat's theme and message. Detailed instructions (including materials needed) are provided for a simple craft that engages the senses and invites hands-on learners to express themselves.

Alternative Craft resources:

For participants who may finish their craft early or are looking for additional ideas, it is helpful to offer additional options. These might include:

- Adult coloring sheets (many can be obtained free online)
- Postcard Project—invite participants to write an inspirational message to themselves based on the retreat's theme, using some of the Scripture verses, quotes, or phrases. Collect the postcards and mail them in four to six weeks as a reminder of their retreat experience.

Suggested Schedule for a Twenty-Four-Hour Retreat:

Create a schedule that is flexible and fits the needs of your group; as events unfold, this may become more of a guideline than a rigidly followed plan. Post the schedule in several places so everyone is clear about time expectations. Remind the group to be good neighbors and to arrive at activities on time so that the group is not waiting for a few stragglers.

Sample Schedule:

Friday

3:00 PM and on—Arrive, settle in; free time.
5:30 PM—Supper
6:30 PM—Introductions and icebreakers
7:30 PM—Group Gathering #1
9:00 PM—Evening Worship
9:30 PM—Free time
10:00 PM—Quiet time

Saturday

7:00 AM—Morning Watch/Quiet Reflection (optional)
8:00 AM—Breakfast, Arrival of Day folks
9:00 AM—Introductions of new arrivals
9:30 AM—Worship
9:45 AM—Group Gathering #2
11:00 AM—Group Gathering #3
12:30 PM—Lunch
1:15 PM—Crafting our message
2:15 PM—Free time
3:30 PM—Worship, sharing, communion
4:30 PM—Head home with renewed spirits; May the Lord keep watch between you and me when we are away from each other (Gen 31:49).

A Word about Friday Evening:

Twenty-four-hour retreats can be tricky if not everyone is able to attend the entire event. Some people will arrive on Saturday morning, eager to start their retreat experience, while those who came on Friday have already immersed themselves in a bonding and learning experience. It is the leader's challenge to bring these two groups together. This can be done by taking time for additional icebreaker exercises on Saturday morning and by offering a brief review of any content covered on Friday evening.

Free Time:

Do not underestimate the value of free time! Unstructured moments can be a rare luxury for many people. It is helpful to offer options—coloring pages, additional craft time, or a labyrinth walk (if available), but don't be surprised if participants choose to go for a short walk, knit, enjoy a conversation, or even take a nap. Any of these activities can be restorative and restful.

As You Begin:

Offer a warm welcome! When everyone has arrived, and is finally gathered in a circle, take a moment before you dive into your program. Pause and look around the circle. Congratulate everyone for being there. Remember that many people engaged in extensive planning and logistics to gain this time away. This is worthy of recognition and celebration! Invite everyone to take a deep breath and perhaps even to give themselves a round of applause. The hard work is completed—they have managed to give themselves the gift of time. Now they can relax, enjoy, and soak up the atmosphere. Encourage participants to limit their use of electronics as much as possible.

Remind participants that they deserve Sabbath rest, not because they are hard-working, compassionate people (although they probably are), but because God wants to give it to them. Sabbath—time away, time to be renewed and restored, time to pray, time to rest—is God's gift to us. It is a gift we are most likely to ignore or even refuse, thinking that we don't need it. Often, people regard taking time off as a sign of weakness or as an undeserved luxury.

Tell them that all of that changes in this moment. The retreat is beginning. Invite everyone to take another deep breath and then to exhale. Encourage them to take a moment to honor this time as sacred. This group of individuals has decided to set aside time for God and for themselves. Well done! Let us now be open to the gifts God wishes to give us in this time and space.

Conclusion:

You're ready! It's time to invite people to come together and create a welcoming atmosphere that reflects God's loving hospitality. For a few hours or a few days, participants can "come away" from society's isolation to experience fellowship and laughter as they listen for God's restoring voice. It's time to create a retreat that will renew and refresh. Enjoy!

Chapter 2

Following the Star

Celebrating Epiphany Together

About This Theme:

Sandwiched between the busy seasons of Advent and Christmas and the more somber, thought-provoking weeks of Lent comes the quiet elation of Epiphany. This joy-filled season shines long after Christmas decorations have been tucked away and New Year's resolutions have fallen to the wayside. The star lingers overhead, inviting us to venture into the unknown. Only when we move beyond the familiar will we encounter the new gifts God is offering.

Epiphany is an often-overlooked but delightful season that offers a light glimmering in the darkness and hope in the midst of despair. It reminds us of the journey of the Magi, who followed mysterious messages to seek God's promise. The star shining overhead cajoles us to leave the safety of our routines behind. The quiet assurance of a God who yearns to be found and who places directional signals in the sky lures us forward.

Unlike Christmas and the New Year, the season of Epiphany is not widely recognized in secular society. January is often regarded with the enthusiasm of a deflated balloon, while the aftermath of Christmas is considered a dreary time to be endured.

This is a golden opportunity for a retreat leader who wishes to share the revelation—the epiphany—of God. This is a season that encourages us to look up, to take time to listen and be aware so that we can, like those ancient travelers, be amazed at what God has to show us.

Most participants will come to this retreat without preconceived ideas of what to expect or how to celebrate. This gives retreat leaders a valuable opportunity, like the wandering Magi, to offer unexpected yet valuable gifts.

Scripture Focus:

- Isaiah 43:1–3a, 4
- Isaiah 60:1–6
- Matthew 2:1–12
- John 1:1–9

"Quotable":

- "Arise, shine; for your light has come" (Isa 60:1).
- "We saw his star when it rose and have come to worship him" (Matt 2:2, NIV).
- "They set out, and there, ahead of them, went the star that they had seen at its rising (Matt 2:9).
- "The light shines in the darkness, and the darkness did not overcome it" (John 1:5).

Introductory Objects and Bring-Along Items:

Invite participants to consider the word "journey" and request that they bring an object to represent that. Explain that a journey may be an actual travel destination, or it may represent a new direction in their life path. Ask them to consider trips that they routinely make (to visit a relative or even local errands) as well as once-in-a-lifetime experiences. What impact have these experiences had, and what would they like to share about those experiences?

Invite participants to contribute any of the craft materials listed in "Crafting Our Message." Send out a list of requested items prior to the retreat.

In addition, encourage participants to bring quotes, short poems, or Scripture verses related to this theme to share during worship and group gatherings. This can be an engaging way to both learn more about one another and expand the repertoire of readings and songs during the retreat.

Music Resources:

Music can be interspersed throughout the retreat at mealtimes, the beginning and conclusion of group gatherings, and during worship.

Hymns:

- "Arise, Your Light Has Come" (tune: "Festal Song"). Inspired by Isaiah 60:1; 61:1–2, the prophet celebrates God's command to shine in this joyous hymn.

- "I Am The Light Of The World!" (tune: "Light of the World"). Howard Thurman's poem "The Work of Christmas" inspired Jim Strathdee to write this lively hymn of encouragement.

- "Lovely Star In The Sky" (tune: "Hanure Binnanun"). This lilting Korean tune celebrates the gifts given to the Christ child and inspires our heartfelt response.

- "Many Are The Lightbeams" (tune: "Lightbeams"). Based on a third-century prayer, this lovely hymn celebrates the diverse expression of the divine light within each of us.

Songs:

- "Behold The Star." An upbeat, hopeful African-American tune that encourages listeners to look "yonder at the star of Bethlehem."

- "Candle On The Water" from *Pete's Dragon* (Disney). Beautiful theme of allowing love to guide us to the light.

- "Do Not Be Afraid, I Am With You" by David Haas. Inspired by Isaiah 43, this song echoes God's loving words of assurance.

- "Go Light Your World" by Chris Rice. Perfect for the season of Epiphany, the song encourages listeners to "take your candle, and go light your world." Inspired by Matthew 5:14–16.

- "Star In The East" by John McCutcheon. Hammer dulcimer and beautiful harmonies tell the inspiring story of Epiphany.
- "The Work of Christmas" by Dan Forrest. Inspired by Howard Thurman's poem with the same name, this haunting melody inspires listeners to live the love of Christmas.

Creating the Atmosphere—Preparing Your Retreat Space:

- Display the schedule for your retreat in several places so it is easily seen by participants.
- Display posters with quotes that you have made.

These items will help convey the star-studded theme of Epiphany:

- Stars! Stars of any shape, color, and size can be used as name tags, posters, or simply as a means to convey the theme.
- Star-shaped "welcome" sign on door.
- Display (star-shaped) posters with biblical quotes that you have made.
- Create a poster with some definitions of the word "epiphany" (look in the dictionary, and on Wikipedia and Google). Leave room on the poster so more definitions can be added during the retreat. The poster can read, "Epiphany is . . ."

Worship Area Suggestions:

When creating a worship area, consider including these items:

- Star-print fabric
- A variety of candles, lanterns, or other light sources. These might be placed on top or in front of a mirror to reflect the light.
- A variety of stars made out of different shapes, sizes, materials; these can be two- or three-dimensional.
- A string of white Christmas or "fairy" lights can be draped across or around the altar table. Alternatively, a string of white lights can be placed inside a tall, clear glass vase for a simple-yet-stunning display of light.

Activities and Discussion Questions for Group Gatherings:

These gatherings can be used in any order, depending on the needs of the group and time constraints.

Group Gathering: Into the Unknown

Background:

As participants consider the Magi's journey, they can reflect on the direction of their own lives.

Materials:

- Used Christmas cards with scenes of Magi, stars, or a journey. There should be a card for every two participants.
- Copies of Matthew 2:1–12 for each person
- Song: "Behold the Star!" or "Arise, Shine, Your Light has Come"
- Five construction paper stars for each person
- Markers
- Reflection questions for each participant

Divide the group into pairs; give each pair a Christmas card. Invite them to look at the card while a volunteer reads Matthew 2:1–12 out loud.

Play a song such as "Behold the Star!" or "Arise, Shine, Your Light has Come."

Tell the group:

> The magi left everything behind in order to follow the star to its unknown location. Going into uncharted territory can be thrilling, disconcerting, frightening, or exhilarating; it depends on the reason for the journey. In our own lives, moving into the unknown is sometimes a choice, and is sometimes forced upon us.

Invite each pair to give their chosen Christmas card a title based on what they consider is being felt or experienced in the picture. After they have had a few moments to discuss this, invite each pair to hold up their card and describe their title.

Now ask the group to consider their own journeys. Ask them to think about new experiences and where they are being led. Provide participants with the following questions:

REFLECTION QUESTIONS:

- What dream(s) would you like to pursue or follow?
- What new experience(s) would you like to have this year?
- What is something new that you are not looking forward to?

Invite them to write their responses on the construction paper stars. They may use several stars to record their answers. After a few moments, divide them into groups (two to four people) and invite them to reflect on their answers.

When everyone has had an opportunity to share, bring the group back together. Invite participants to reflect on their star journeys. With their permission, the stars can be hung up as a visual reminder of the journeys we are all experiencing. This paper star constellation can offer food for thought for additional group gatherings.

Group Gathering: Overcoming Obstacles

Background:

The story of the magi reminds us of obstacles and challenges we have confronted along our life journey.

Materials:

- Newsprint labeled "Emotions of Herod"
- Newsprint labeled "Emotions of Magi"
- Markers
- Tape

- Copies of Matthew 2:1–12 for each participant
- Discussion questions for each participant
- Pens for each participant
- Song: "Behold the Star"

Invite the group to listen to the song "Behold the Star." Ask the group to give one- or two-word answers to the question, "What message do you hear in this song?"

Tell the group:

> We will be exploring the story of the Magi's journey and discovering what we might learn for our own path. As we listen to the Magi's story, consider what kind of emotions they might have experienced along the way.

Invite a volunteer to read Matthew 2:1–12 out loud.
Tell the group:

> This story portrays the conflict between the Magi and King Herod. They had differing purposes and agendas. Herod pretended to share the Magi's goal of wanting to worship this newborn king, while he secretly only wanted to destroy him.

Invite the group to brainstorm the variety of emotions that the Magi and Herod had, encouraging them to explore the range of feelings that each person might have been experiencing in that tumultuous time (for example, the wise men weren't simply "wise" or "brave"; they may also have been frightened, unsure, excited, and so on). Ask volunteers to record the group's responses on the prepared newsprint.

Tell the group that we can use these lists of emotions to reflect on experiences of our own. Invite them to use the discussion questions to reflect on their own life journey and to write down their responses.

DISCUSSION QUESTIONS:

- When was a time you had to take a risk to follow a dream?

- Some people might have considered the Magi to be foolish or misguided. Have you had a dream or goal that no one else seemed to share or understand? What was it? What kept you focused?

- Have you had the experience of leaving the familiar behind in order to venture out into the unknown? Is there something you would like to leave behind now?

- The Magi stopped to ask for directions. Who has offered you support or guidance along your journey?

- What was some of the best help or advice you have received? Have you had any Herod-like, bad advice?

- King Herod was furious when the Magi ignored his instructions. How do you deal with naysayers or those who seem to discourage your dreams?

After individual reflection, divide the participants into small groups to discuss their responses.

Group Gathering: Seeking and Sharing the Light

Background:

The prophet Isaiah rejoices in God's light shining in the darkness. Participants can consider where God's light is shining today. Each of us can act as a light-bearer as we share God's hope.

Materials:

- Copies of Isaiah 60:1–4 in a variety of translations
- Song: "Go Light Your World" and "Many Are The Lightbeams"
- Newsprint
- Markers
- Tape
- Discussion questions for each small group

Tell the group that they will be considering God's light, which provides hope in the darkness. Let them know that the prophet Isaiah is speaking to the people of Israel after a long period of war and suffering; Isaiah is finally offering words of hope and encouragement to people who are parched and weary.

Ask volunteers to read translations of the Isaiah passage. Between each reading you may choose to sing a verse of the hymn "Many Are The Lightbeams" or to listen to sections of a song.

Ask the group to name those who especially need to hear these words of hope today. Invite participants to consider people known to them, as well as those in the news. Have a volunteer record their answers.

Invite the group to listen to the song "Go Light Your World." Divide the participants into small groups and invite them to discuss these questions:

DISCUSSION QUESTIONS:

- Where do we see signs of God's light and hope?
- The Magi followed the star, Joseph listened to a dream, the shepherds heard the angels. How does God speak to us today?
- The Magi followed the light of the star. How do we know what is the right direction for our lives?
- Isaiah is filled with joy when he says, "Arise, shine, for your light has come" (Isaiah 60:1). What fills your heart with joy? What lifts your spirits and offers hope?

Group Gathering: Accordion Poem

Background:

This activity encourages participants to respond to the light and hope of Epiphany through a creative group effort.

Materials:

- Paper for each group
- Pens
- Epiphany song of your choice

18

Activity:

Remind participants that the season of Epiphany is about our response to God's gifts. Mary and Joseph respond faithfully to God's guidance, while the Magi travel long distances to discover the star-lit gift of the child. This activity allows participants to work together to respond to God's gifts.

Form groups with seven to eight participants. Provide each group with a piece of paper, held lengthwise. Invite participants to listen to an Epiphany song to remind them of the joyful themes of this season.

Each group will create an "accordion poem" about Epiphany. The first person in the group will write one line about Epiphany. This can be about the song they just heard, about the Epiphany season as a whole, or about specific characters or aspects about Epiphany.

The second person will write a line under the first. This second line should follow logically to the first; it may continue the same theme or add to it.

Before the third person receives the paper, the top line must be folded back so that only the second line is visible. The third person writes a line and then folds the paper forward so that only the line they wrote is visible. Each participant only sees the line written by the previous person.

This continues until every participant in the group has written a line.

When the groups have completed their Epiphany poems, invite them to unfold the paper and read the entire poem to the group.

This lighthearted exercise reminds participants that God's Spirit can weave in and through our lives in mysterious ways.

Group Gathering: Star Gifts

Background:

This activity is inspired by the Magi's star-led journey to Bethlehem, where gifts were exchanged. The travelers offered Jesus gold, frankincense, and myrrh. In return, they received the life-changing experience of witnessing God's gift of love embodied in a baby.

Star gifts remind us that God is always offering us messages of encouragement and wisdom. These gifts are words printed on cut-out stars that provide thoughtful inspiration for the recipient.

This exercise can easily be shared with the entire congregation; it is a positive way to share a portion of the retreat experience with others. In some congregations (including my own) "Star Gift Sunday" is a beloved annual tradition on Epiphany Sunday. Everyone receives a star with a word to ponder for the coming year; these inspire thoughtful conversations and reflections.

Materials:

- Star gifts (words printed on cutout stars). The list of words is below
- Matthew 2:11

Activity:

Remind the group that the magi offered Jesus gifts by reading Matthew 2:11. You may like to have a discussion about what these gifts are and what their significance might be.

Ask the group to discuss gifts they have received over the years. Engage in conversation with these questions:

REFLECTION QUESTIONS:

- What is the best, worst, or most meaningful gift you have received?
- What makes something a joy to receive?

Ask the group to think about gifts they have given. This might be more challenging for some people who are reticent about discussing their own actions or generosity. Frame the question in a way that encourages participants to think about a gift that they felt good about giving. What inspired them to offer that gift? What was the response?

Tell the group:

> While Christmas is the celebration of God's gift to us in Jesus, Epiphany reminds us of the lingering effects of that gift. The season of Epiphany lasts for weeks following Christmas as a recognition that God's Light remains with us. We will listen to a song that tells the story of the magi and Epiphany.

Play the song "Lovely Star In The Sky" or "Star In The East."

Tell the group that they will receive a "star gift." Each star contains a word from a list of over a hundred words. Each person will randomly select a star gift to take home and reflect on in the coming months. They should hang the word up where it will be seen often—on the computer, mirror, refrigerator.

Here are some "guidelines" for receiving star gifts:

- The word that you choose is your word. It can't be traded for another.

- If you don't understand the meaning or significance of the word, don't be frustrated. It is an invitation to wonder about it and learn from it. You have the word for an entire year; take time to look it up or to see how it is used in different contexts.

- Don't assume you know what your word signifies. Ask questions about your word and wonder what it has to say to you. For example, if a generous person receives the word "generosity," it may become an invitation to receive, and not only give, acts of kindness.

- It can be fun/interesting to set a reminder in your calendar to look at your word again in future months. Your life will be in a different place and your word might take on new meaning.

Pass out the star gifts to everyone. Break into small groups (three to six people) to discuss the star words and their possible meanings. It can be helpful to take time with each word and brainstorm possible meanings and insights.

Listen to an Epiphany song of your choice to close this gathering.

STAR GIFTS:

kindness	caring	sharing	giving	compassion
love	openness	pardon	understanding	discipleship
servanthood	stability	hopefulness	innocence	prayerfulness
praise	gentleness	knowledge	happiness	laughter
acceptance	self-control	restraint	mercy	truth
peace	faith	consideration	fellowship	unity
teaching	singing	celebration	perseverance	judgment
discipline	courage	confidence	clarity	honor
contentment	imagination	commitment	friendship	freedom

creativity	devotion	joy	strength	comfort
leadership	discernment	obedience	thoughtfulness	responsibility
patience	forgiveness	humility	faithfulness	hope
tenderness	enthusiasm	evangelism	healing	loyalty
rejoicing	respect	insight	selflessness	righteousness
assurance	justice	honesty	wisdom	awareness
tolerance	wholeness	guidance	hospitality	foresight
trust	learning	proclamation	encouragement	trustworthiness
inspiration	wonder	flexibility	grace	graciousness
integrity	helping	witnessing	generosity	perceptiveness
purity	prayer	service	steadfastness	determination
nurturing	renewal	purpose	peacefulness	power
excitement	harmony	reliability	goodness	reverence
serenity	humor	boldness	genuineness	illumination
vision	dependability	endurance	listening	accountability
speaking	sincerity	writing	music	motivation
art	building	crafts	planning	organization
drama	cheerfulness	focus	balance	helpfulness
languages	cooking	sympathy	empathy	sensitivity
time	conviction	delight	responsiveness	education
intelligence	experience	visitation	sobriety	spirituality
travel	thankfulness	money	dignity	quietness
playfulness	dedication	empathy	solitude	zeal
appreciation	affirmation	charity		

Crafting Our Message: Creating a Gift for Ourselves

Purpose:

Inspired by the Magi's gifts, participants will create a decorated box. Through reflection and sharing, participants can consider gifts and blessings received from God.

Materials:

- Boxes, a variety of shapes and sizes (tobacco shops often have free or inexpensive cigar boxes)
- Variety of glue types—for paper and other materials
- Glue guns for gluing bigger items
- Materials to decorate boxes (see list below)
- Tissue paper
- Ribbon

This is an opportunity to crowdsource the materials necessary for this craft. Not only will this reduce the expense of the craft, it will also provide a greater diversity of materials. None of the materials need to be new, perfect, or complete. The craft reinforces the concept that God accepts and uses us just as we are. Participants will discover what they can cobble together with the materials at hand.

Invite your participants to bring along any craft or art supplies they may have. Be receptive to whatever people might offer, which might include:

- Paints
- Markers
- Beads
- Feathers
- Photos
- Magazine or calendar pictures
- Used greeting cards
- Rocks
- Fabric
- Yarn
- Stickers
- And so on. The sky is the limit!

Directions:

1. Look at the variety of boxes. Take time to notice the differences between them. Choose one that appeals to you.

2. Look at the variety of craft materials available. Use them to decorate your box, inside and out.

3. Invite participants to reflect on these questions:

   - What significance do the decorations on the box have?
   - What items would you keep in this box?
   - What has value to you?
   - What do you consider precious or wish to preserve?
   - What blessings have you received from God?

When everyone has completed the craft, invite participants to describe their box to the group, answering as many of the questions as they choose.

Optional: Invite everyone to wrap their box in tissue paper, adding a bow if desired. Tell them that they can open their gift to themselves at the end of Epiphany (or in several weeks, whichever is longer). Reflect on the giving and receiving of gifts.

The completed boxes can be added to the worship area to remind participants of God's gifts.

Additional Craft Resources (for those who complete the craft early and are looking for further ideas):

- Adult coloring sheets (can be obtained free online)
- Colored pencils
- Pre-stamped postcards and pens (to be mailed by leader six to eight weeks after the retreat). Participants can write themselves a short note highlighting meaningful moments or quotes from the retreat.

Worship Resources:

These are themed resources for this particular retreat. Additional resources are available in the Appendix.

Unison prayer:

Star of Wonder, You bring light and life to a world in need of your healing, your grace, and your unwavering love. Whether our eyes are open and eager with anticipation to discover all you are prepared to reveal or whether we are squinting cautiously through eyes uncertain of all we are invited to behold, you welcome us into your presence. Help us to receive Love's blinding light so that we may know something more of who you are and all you offer our lives in this season of awe. Help us to dare to receive your light and then to share it. Amen.

—Karen Ziel

Litany:

Leader: Arise, your light is come! God's glory shines all around us.

People: Arise, your light is come! God's Spirit is calling to us today and every day.

Leader: Arise, God's light is with us. God's light shines and even the darkness cannot destroy it.

People: Arise, let us be filled with God's light. Let us say yes to God's gifts and guidance.

Chapter 3

Self-Care

Tending to Our Spirit

About This Theme:

This retreat offers a reprieve for busy people living in a twenty-four seven society running on hyperdrive. The world does not slow down, and rarely offers a respite to feed our souls. Society provides little encouragement to rest; we need to claim that for ourselves.

When we ask someone how they are, we often hear the joyless reply, "I am busy." Many people are tired of running around, being overbooked, endlessly caring for children or elders, staring at computer screens, shouldering responsibilities at work, school, church, and volunteer organizations. People are exhausted by a war-torn world filled with a seemingly endless stream of bad news. We carry on relentlessly, endlessly endeavoring to fulfill our responsibilities until we finally realize, as the hymn "Precious Lord, Take my Hand" laments, "I am tired, I am weak, I am worn."

It is time for some comfort for the soul. This retreat offers a virtual pause button that allows participants time and space to gain perspective on their lives. This is not about running away from problems and concerns, but rather about remembering God's promise to sustain us. Participants will discover the freedom that comes from. Participants will discover strategies to nurture their spirits every day as they experience the joy of supporting one another along life's journey.

Scripture Focus:

- Isaiah 43:1–5
- Psalm 46
- Psalm 62:1–8
- Matthew 26:6–13
- Luke 19:1–10

"Quotable":

- "God is our refuge and strength, a very present help in time of trouble." (Ps 46:1).
- "God is my rock and salvation" (Ps 62:2).
- "The Lord is near to all who call on him" (Ps 145:18).
- "Do not fear, for I am with you" (Isa 43:5).
- "Come to me all you who are weary and carrying heavy burdens and I will give you rest" (Matt 11:28).
- "Do not worry about anything, but in everything by prayer and supplication with thanksgiving let your requests be made known to God" (Phil 4:6).
- "Be strong enough to stand alone, smart enough to know when you need help, and brave enough to ask for it."—Anonymous
- "No one cares how much you know, until they know how much you care."—Theodore Roosevelt

Introductory Objects and Bring-Along Items:

Invite participants to bring an object that signifies a way they connect with God, a reminder of God's presence, or a way that they relax and soothe their spirits. This broad invitation should result in a wide variety of responses that can provide rich food for thought and fodder for conversation.

In addition, encourage participants to bring quotes, short poems, or Scripture verses related to this theme to share during worship and group gatherings.

Crowdsource craft materials from participants (see "Crafting Our Message"). People who knit, stamp, paint, or engage in other crafts may be willing to share supplies to enable others to experiment with this craft form.

Leader's Tip:

Consider your own experience establishing healthy self-care. Be prepared to share struggles as well as successful practices with participants.

If any of the participants leads yoga or other relaxation exercises, invite them to share a short introduction.

Music Resources:

Music can be interspersed throughout the retreat at mealtimes, the beginning and conclusion of group gatherings, and during worship.

Hymns:

- "A Mighty Fortress Is Our God" (tune: "Ein' Feste Burg"). Inspired by Psalm 46, this powerful song celebrates God's strength and faithfulness.

- "How Can I Keep From Singing?" (tune: "Endless Song"). Despite hardship and loss, the lyrics compel us to keep trusting God's faithfulness.

- "What A Friend We Have In Jesus" (tune: "Erie"). This reassuring hymn urges us to take "everything to God in prayer" to receive needed wisdom and insight.

Songs:

- "Be Still And Know That I Am God." Several versions of this simple song exist, inviting listeners to pause and become aware of God's presence.

- "Comfort My People" by Monica Brown. This beautiful song acknowledges life's painful passages while God reassures, "I, myself, will lead them through the darkness."

- "Dona Nobis Pacem (Give us Peace)." Many versions of this beautiful round are available to help listeners sing and pray.

- "His Eye Is On The Sparrow" sung by Whitney Houston. Although this song is included in many hymnals, it is not always easy to sing. Houston's stunning rendition highlights God's compassion and promise to be with us.

- "Precious Lord Take My Hand." Mahalia Jackson's version offers a heartfelt plea for God's strength.

- "Three Little Birds" by Bob Marley. Words of reassurance reminding us not to be consumed by worry.

Creating the Atmosphere—Preparing Your Retreat Space:

As much as possible in your retreat space, try to create a homey, comfortable atmosphere. This might include fresh flowers, making available comfortable pillows and prayer shawls, and a tea/coffee corner. Beginning each group gathering with music can help calm the atmosphere and encourage participants to relax.

Worship Area Suggestions:

When creating a worship area, these items might be included:

- Candles
- Bowl of water
- Flowers
- Soft fabric

Activities and Discussion Questions for Group Gatherings:

These gatherings can be used in any order, depending on the needs of the group and time constraints.

Group Gathering: Defining "Rest"

Background:

Jesus said, "Come to me, all you that are weary and are carrying heavy burdens, and I will give you rest" (Matt 11:28); this group exercise allows participants to define what "comfort" and "rest" mean to them.

Materials:

- Newsprint, each with one letter to spell R-E-S-T
- Marker for each participant
- Psalm 46 for each participant
- Matthew 11:28
- Song: "Precious Lord, Take My Hand"
- Discussion questions

Activity:

Read Matthew 11:28 to the group. Tell them:

> We are going to explore what it means to need the rest and comfort God offers to us. The hymn "Precious Lord, Take My Hand" is an emotional plea by someone who is weary and yearning for God's help and support. As you listen to it, think about what why you might need the rest that God offers.

Invite the group to sing or listen to the song "Precious Lord, Take My Hand." Tell the group:

> The theme of needing God's rest and help is found throughout the Bible. Psalm 46 is a powerful song that defines God as "refuge" and "strength." The psalmist describes moments of complete chaos, but then invites listeners to "be still" so that we can become aware of God's presence. We will listen to the psalm and then define the rest that God wishes to give to us.

Ask a volunteer to read Psalm 46 as the group follows along. Engage the participants in conversation with these questions:

DISCUSSION QUESTIONS:

1. How would you define the word "refuge"? The word "refugee" is more often heard these days than "refuge." How do you think they are related?

2. When do we need God's strength?

3. The psalmist says that God changes everything; wars end and weapons are destroyed so that peace can prevail. What would we like to ask God to do?

We will be thinking about the word "rest" as we consider the gifts God offers to us. Say to the group:

> Think about why rest might be needed and why God wants to offer that. What would rest look or feel like in your life? What gifts does God offer us? How does God invite us to rest? Write those words or phrases on the newsprint. The answers should correspond with the title letter. Words on the "R" page should start with the letter "r," words on the "E" page should begin with the letter "e" and so on.

When the participants have finished writing, ask volunteers to read the words from one sheet at a time. Take the time to ask for reactions to the responses. Write any additional words that arise during the discussion.

Leave the newsprint up as food for thought throughout the retreat.

You may choose to play the same or another song to conclude this gathering.

Group Gathering: Caring For Others—and Yourself

Background:

Matthew 26:6–13 gives us a rare glimpse of Jesus being cared for by someone else. We are familiar with Jesus the powerful preacher who captivates a crowd of thousands, who conquers a storm by walking on water, and who performs miracles by raising a little girl from her deathbed. This story allows us to view a weary Jesus who is willing to be cared for by an unnamed woman. He appreciates her tender concern as she pours valuable ointment on his head. While the disciples attempt to thwart her efforts, Jesus welcomes her kindness. Jesus honors her loving actions by saying, "She has done a beautiful thing to me" (Matt 26:10).

Materials:

- Newsprint and markers
- Matthew 26:6–13
- Discussion questions for each participant

Activity:

Begin this activity by inviting the group to offer words that describe Jesus. Encourage them to think about his characteristics and activities. Record their answers on newsprint.

Tell the group that this Gospel story offers additional information about Jesus which provides a more vulnerable side.

Ask a volunteer to read Matthew 26:6–13 to the group. Engage participants in conversation with the following questions:

DISCUSSION QUESTIONS:

- Just prior to this story, Jesus had been teaching crowds of followers. Jesus knew that many people "conspired to arrest [him] by stealth and kill him" (Matthew 25:4). It is no wonder that he was weary! Does an image of Jesus who appreciates the care and concern of another alter your opinion of him?
- Why do you think the disciples objected to the woman's actions?
- Why do you think the woman approached Jesus to pour the oil?

Pass out copies of the following discussion questions. Provide time for the participants to write answers to these questions individually. When they have completed the questions, divide into small groups to discuss their responses.

DISCUSSION QUESTIONS:

1. What are times when you have physically cared for another person?

2. Who are you caring for or worrying about right now?

3. Are there times when you—like Jesus—realize that you need help, support, and love?

4. Are you able to accept the care of others?

5. What burdens would you like to lay aside right now or have someone help you with?

6. The woman in Matthew 26 acts according to the custom of her time; she cares for Jesus by anointing him with oil. What kind of care would you like to receive? What action would show you consideration and love?

Conclude this group gathering by listening to "How Can I Keep From Singing?"

Group Gathering: Immersing Ourselves in Silence

Background:

Silence is a rare commodity in our media-saturated world. One way to soothe our spirits is to shut out that noise and immerse ourselves in silence. This is a time when nothing needs to be produced or accomplished; participants have the freedom to simply experience this unplanned time. It is an invitation to be aware of God's presence and to welcome God's Spirit.

Offering some optional quiet activities such as drawing materials or a jigsaw puzzle will be helpful for some people who may not be completely comfortable with silence.

Materials:

- Songs: "Be Still and Know That I Am God," "Dona Nobis Pacem"
- Create a handout for each participant entitled "Meeting God in Silence" by printing the following Scriptures: Psalm 46; Psalm 62:1–8; Matthew 14:23; Mark 1:35; Luke 5:15–16.

- Pen for each participant
- Optional quiet activities, such as drawing materials, jigsaw puzzle, books
- Reflection questions
- Bell or whistle

Activity:

Say to the group:

> The gospels give many examples of Jesus seeking out a quiet place; we are told that he "would withdraw to deserted places and pray" (Luke 5:16). Psalm 46:10 encourages us to "be still and know that I am God." This will be an opportunity to experience an unplanned, unscheduled hour enjoying a period of silence. There is nothing you need to do or accomplish during this time.

Explain to the group that this song is inspired by Psalm 46.
Play the song "Be Still And Know That I Am God."
Say to the group:

> Now it is our opportunity to be still and spend some time entering into silence. During these moments, take time to engage your five senses and really notice your surroundings. You might want to look around and notice as much as you can about where you are. Ask yourself, "What do I hear? Is there an odor? What can I feel?"
>
> Some readings are being provided in case you would like some food for thought, but reading is not required. This time of intentional silence is a chance to unwind and be aware of how God may be speaking to you.

Explain to the group that they may choose where to experience the silence; they may remain in the room or find another area (define the boundaries/parameters of your location). Point out options for how to use this time; they may simply experience the silence or engage in one of the quiet activities. Tell the group how long the silence will be (I suggest an hour to allow participants time to settle down and enter into the experience).

Before the time of silence begins, ask if there are any questions. Tell the group:

> I will play the song "Dona Nobis Pacem" (which means "give us peace"). At the end of the song, you are invited to begin your experience of silence. I will use this noisemaker to indicate when it is time to re-gather.

Invite the group to sit comfortably as they listen to "Dona Nobis Pacem."

When the group returns, invite them to reflect on their experience with these questions:

REFLECTION QUESTIONS:

- How was your experience with silence?
- Was the amount of time too short? Too long?
- Would it be helpful to incorporate silence into your daily life?
- Did the silence inspire you to consider practices that might offer you peace?

Group Gathering: Offering Words of Encouragement

Background:

This activity allows participants to both give and receive comfort and support.

Materials:

- Brown paper lunch bag for each participant
- Set of index cards for each participant
- Pens, markers

- Song: "Comfort My People"
- Copies of Reader's Theater Luke 19:1–10

Activity:

Ask the group:

> What is easier for you—to give comfort to someone or to receive comfort from someone else? Why is that?
>
> We will be considering the power of offering one another comfort. There are periods in our lives when we simply need the help and support of others. There are other times when we can respond with compassion to someone else's distress or sadness.

Divide into groups of eight to ten people. Invite everyone to take a brown paper lunch bag and label it with their name. Encourage them to decorate or color the bag to personalize it as they wish. When everyone has labeled a bag, place each group's bags together on a table with the names facing outward.

As you prepare to play the song "Comfort My People," let the group know that this song describes God's compassion for those in need and encourages us to reflect God's love to God's people.

Play "Comfort My People."

Tell the group:

> As we think about God's compassion, we will hear this Gospel story which depicts Jesus reaching out to someone who does not even ask for help. Jesus recognizes his despair and responds with forgiveness, community, and compassion.

Ask volunteers to participate in the Reader's Theater of Luke 19:1–10. Engage the group in conversation with the following questions:

REFLECTION QUESTIONS:

- Why did Zacchaeus go to such lengths to see Jesus? What do you think he hoped would happen?

- Why do you think Jesus spoke to Zacchaeus?
- Why was the crowd unhappy with Jesus' actions? Why did the crowd grumble?

Tell the group:

> God has placed us in each other's lives so we can offer help, encouragement, and support. We are invited to share some caring words right now. Everyone is invited to write a message of encouragement for each of the participants in our small groups and place it in the paper bags. You have choices—you can write the same message to each person or personalize it depending on the recipient. You may compose an original message or share a meaningful quote or Scripture passage. Write the message on an index card and place it in the brown paper bags.

When the group has accomplished this task (but before they have read the messages in their bag), invite them to reflect on the experience with these questions:

REFLECTION QUESTIONS:

- How did it feel to offer support to one another in this way?
- Do you consider yourself to be someone who is able to offer comfort? How do you do that?
- Can you think of a time when you have received support from another? What was that experience like?
- Jesus' had the ability to identify Zacchaeus' need. Is it possible for us to develop the gift of empathy and caring?

At the conclusion of the conversation, play the song "Comfort My People" again. Provide time for participants to read the messages they have received. Although they need not share the messages, some may wish to offer some of the quotes or words of comfort during worship.

You may choose to leave the bags available so participants may give additional messages to those not in their original small group.

Readers' Theater: Luke 19:1–10

Narrator: Jesus entered Jericho and was passing through it. A man was there named Zacchaeus; he was a chief tax collector and was rich. He was trying to see who Jesus was, but on account of the crowd he could not, because he was short in stature. So he ran ahead and climbed a sycamore tree to see him, because he was going to pass that way. When Jesus came to the place, he looked up and said to him,

Jesus: "Zacchaeus, hurry and come down; for I must stay at your house today."

Narrator: So he hurried down and was happy to welcome him. All who saw it began to grumble and said,

Crowd: "He has gone to be the guest of one who is a sinner."

Narrator: Zacchaeus stood there and said to the Lord,

Zacchaeus: "Look, half of my possessions, Lord, I will give to the poor; and if I have defrauded anyone of anything, I will pay back four times as much."

Jesus: "Today salvation has come to this house, because he too is a son of Abraham. For the Son of Man came to seek out and to save the lost."

Group Gathering: Our Psalm of Comfort

Background:

Psalm 62 is prayer for help and strength. The psalmist uses powerful words to describe distress; the writer "thirsts," "faints," and is in a "dry and weary land." This activity helps participants reflect on challenging circumstances while searching for God's promised help.

Materials:

- Psalm 62 (NIV) with reflection questions for each participant
- Pens
- Newsprint and marker

- Song: "His Eye Is On The Sparrow"

Activity, Part 1:

Tell the group:

> There has never been a time in history when people haven't needed help and support in their lives. We can learn from the ancient writing found in the psalm about how to talk about those difficult times and then how to turn to God for help.
>
> We will look at sections of Psalm 62 to explore why we need comfort and how comfort can be found. The psalmist identifies his troubles and concerns but expresses faith that God is still there.
>
> First, we will talk about the psalm together. After our conversation, everyone will be invited to write their own psalm, using the outline of Psalm 62.

Ask a volunteer to read one section of the psalm at a time. Pause after each section to discuss the listed questions. Enlist a volunteer to record the responses on newsprint.

Psalm 62 (NIV)

STATEMENT OF FAITH = THIS IS WHERE TO FIND COMFORT

> Truly my soul finds rest in God;
> my salvation comes from him.
> Truly he is my rock and my salvation;
> he is my fortress, I will never be shaken. (vv. 1–2)

REFLECTION QUESTIONS:

- What does it feel like to "find rest in God"?
- The psalmist names God as "salvation," "rock," "fortress." What names do you call God? How do you describe God?
- "Rock" and "fortress" are words of strength. When do you need God to be strong?

The Problem = Why I Need Comfort

> How long will you assault me?
> Would all of you throw me down—
> this leaning wall, this tottering fence?
> Surely they intend to topple me
> from my lofty place;
> they take delight in lies.
> With their mouths they bless,
> but in their hearts they curse. (vv. 3–4)

Reflection Questions:

- The psalmist is listing fears and concerns. The writer doesn't hold back—it's a very honest list. This means we can say anything to God. We can be honest about what we are feeling and experiencing. As a group, let's list some fears that we might bring to God.

- The psalmist seems to fear that they will always be weighed down by troubles and that this pain may never end. When might someone feel like that?

The Invitation = This is What I Need

> Yes, my soul, find rest in God;
> my hope comes from him. (v. 5)

Reflection Questions:

- What helps you rest? What is relaxing for you?
- Where do you go or what do you do to be more aware of God?
- How can God give us "rest" and "hope"?

The Reason = This is What God is Like

> Truly he is my rock and my salvation;
> he is my fortress, I will not be shaken.
> My salvation and my honor depend on God;
> he is my mighty rock, my refuge.

Trust in him at all times, you people;
pour out your hearts to him,
for God is our refuge. (v. 6–8)

REFLECTION QUESTIONS:

- A "refuge" is a safe place. Where is a refuge for you?

- The psalmist uses words like "rock" and "fortress" to describe God. Are those words meaningful to you? What other words might you use to describe God? Everyone might imagine God a bit differently. Let's make a list with as many words as we can.

- If you could take a break from one or two of your responsibilities for a short time (without any harm being done), which ones would you choose?

- The psalmist "will not be shaken." Do you ever have that kind of confidence? Where did you learn it? Did you have a role model who was very confident? What helps you be strong?

At the conclusion of this conversation, offer a "stretch break" with optional music before continuing with Part 2.

Activity, Part 2:

Gather the group back together with the song "His Eye Is On The Sparrow" or another song of your choice.

Say to the group:

> Now that we have explored Psalm 62 together, you are invited to write your own psalm based on your experiences. Psalm 62 is our model, but it is just an example; you don't need to try to "copy" the psalm or make it sound formal or finished. Simply respond to the questions in each section to create your personal statement.

My Psalm

1. Statement of Faith = This is Where to Find Comfort
   Where do you find comfort? Write some sentences to give thanks for those places of refuge.

2. The Problem = Why I Need Comfort
   Describe what is worrying you and weighing you down.
   Talk about people or circumstances that form a knot in your stomach.

3. The Invitation = This is What I Need
   What do you yearn for? What kind of help or support do you need?
   Tell God what kind of help you desire.

4. The Reason = This is What God is Like
   Write some things you know about God (for example: God, I know you are . . .)
   If possible, express confidence in God.
   Or, describe your hope that you will discover more about God in your situation.

Allow participants enough time to compose their psalm (depending on the group, this might be fifteen to thirty minutes). You may wish to play quiet music in the background. Set a time for the group to reconvene; some participants may desire privacy to compose their psalm.

When the group returns, engage them in conversation with these questions:

REFLECTION QUESTIONS:

- What was the experience of writing your own psalm like? Was it helpful, challenging, eye-opening?
- Did you gain any insights through this process?
- Could writing or journaling offer comfort to you in your daily life? If not, what else might help you reflect on challenges you may face?

Divide into small groups and invite participants to share as much of their psalms as they wish. Participants might choose to share parts of their psalm during worship time.

This group gathering can be concluded by listening or singing to "His Eye Is On The Sparrow" or another song of your choice.

Crafting Our Message: Crafting Smorgasbord

Background:

Simple crafts can engage our hands while allowing our minds to mull over questions or concerns. Crafting can be a form of prayer; our hands can be busy while our hearts communicate with God.

Purpose:

Explore a variety of hands-on activities to discover paths to enjoyment or peace of mind. Participants may discover an activity that they will continue at home.

Some options might include:

- Adult coloring pages (need pages from the Internet or books, colored pencils)
- Writing letters (need notecards, pens)
- Decorating the altar (need objects from nature)
- Knitting (need needles, yarn, a willing teacher)
- Painting rocks; because "God is my rock and my salvation" (Psalm 62:2), participants can paint designs or quotes on rocks. Materials: smooth stones, small paintbrushes, paint, permanent markers)
- Other craft activities brought by participants (for example: stamping)

Activity:

Set up a series of stations with craft materials and simple instructions. Encourage participants to try a variety of craft forms as they explore ways to soothe their spirits and calm their minds.

Say to the group:

> You have the freedom to try as many of these activities as you choose. You do not have to be "good" at any of them. The idea is to experiment with a variety of craft forms as you search for one that helps you relax or enables you to free your creative energy. As you try each craft, be aware of your experience—how are you feeling? Are you engaging in something new or revisiting a familiar activity? How does this activity affect your mood or state of mind?

Let the group know how much time is allotted for this activity. When time is up, gather the group together to reflect on their experience. Engage in conversation with the following questions:

REFLECTION QUESTIONS:

- Which activity did you particularly enjoy?
- Do you prefer these activities in a group or on your own?
- Are there any of these activities that you can imagine doing on your own after the retreat?

Additional Craft Resources (for those who complete the craft early and are looking for further ideas):

- Adult coloring sheets (can be obtained free online)
- Colored pencils
- Pre-stamped postcards and pens (to be mailed by leader six to eight weeks after the retreat). Participants can write themselves a short note highlighting meaningful moments or quotes from the retreat.

Worship Resources:

These are themed resources to go with this particular retreat. Additional resources are available in the Appendix.

Litanies

LITANY (INSPIRED BY PSALM 46 AND "A MIGHTY FORTRESS IS OUR GOD")

> Leader: We celebrate God, our refuge and our strength.
>
> People: We worship God, a loving presence in times of trouble.
>
> Leader: Even amidst great change, when mountains shake and waters roar and foam,
>
> People: We will not fear, for our everlasting, faithful God is an ever-present help.

LITANY (INSPIRED BY LUKE 19:1–10)

> Leader: "Hurry and come down, Zacchaeus, I must stay at your house today."
>
> People: Jesus' invitation soothed an outsider's heart.
>
> Leader: Come down to community. Come down to forgiveness.
>
> People: Let us say yes and receive God's comforting love.
>
> Leader: Come down to welcome. Come down to new life.
>
> People: God meets us where we are, offering healing and peace.

Unison prayers

I'm a bit overwhelmed, Lord. My to-do list is long. My worry list is even longer. My mind is racing, yet my feet are not moving. Stuck in anxiety, trapped by fear, and filled with doubt, I don't know what to do next. Where do I even begin? Yet you promise to be my rock. That sounds like strength. You assure me with your comfort. That sounds like hope. You offer me quiet in the midst of the storm. That sounds like rest. Filled with your gifts and soothed by your compassion, guide me day by day and moment by moment. Help me listen for your quiet voice so I can receive your comfort and then share your love. Amen.

The news is grim, loving God. We can hardly bear to listen. There are daily accounts of war and terror, people adrift seeking safety and shelter, natural disasters devastating the vulnerable, reports of violence, hunger, and homelessness. It's tempting to dive under the covers, hide our heads, and ignore what we don't seem to be able to fix. Yet, God of comfort, you call us—first to receive your healing presence, then to share your compassion. God of all people, even as we despair at what we can't do, inspire us to offer what we are able. Help us love our neighbors, the ones far away and the ones right next to us. With acts of kindness, words of caring, and hearts filled with welcoming grace, help us be bearers of your comfort as we share your hope and new life. Amen.

Chapter 4

Discovering Our Voices

Exploring the Adventures of Esther

About This Theme:

Esther is a biblical superhero. She is a model of courage who stares down bullies, speaks up to power, fights for justice, and steps out in faith to face her fears. This action-packed biblical account is filled with characters who inspire us to discover our voice and celebrate our (often undervalued) abilities.

The book of Esther inspires each of us to serve God, even in daunting circumstances. The diversity of gifts found in God's people allows each one to express faith and conviction by different, yet effective, means. We will see Vashti, who demonstrates remarkable backbone and strength of spirit as she conveys faith and dignity. Mordecai refuses to compromise his beliefs, even when threatened with power that can annihilate him and the people he loves. Mordecai and Esther support one another under adverse conditions and discover their strength and God's faithfulness.

This retreat will inspire participants to marvel that God is calling each one of us to live our faith for "such a time as this." By immersing themselves in the story of Esther, participants will be empowered to reflect on how to answer God's call in their own life journey.

Scripture Focus:

- Esther 2–8: Since this is a lengthy story, you can encourage participants to read the story prior to the retreat. They can read from an
adult Bible, or you can send them a link to a simplified version at
dltk-kids.com or biblewise.com

- 1 Corinthians 12:4–18

"Quotable":

- "Who knows? Perhaps you have come . . . for just such a time as this"
(Esth 4:14).

- "Shout it aloud, do not hold back. Raise your voice like a trumpet"
(Isa 55:1).

- "Oh, sing to the LORD a new song; sing to the LORD, all the earth!"
(Ps 96:1).

- "You are the light of the world . . . No one after lighting a lamp puts it
under the bushel basket" (Matt 5:14–15).

- "God's various expressions of power are in action everywhere; but
God himself is behind it all. Each person is given something to do
that shows who God is: Everyone gets in on it, everyone benefits" (1
Cor 12:5–6, MSG).

- "There is no greater agony than bearing an untold story inside you."
—Maya Angelou

Introductory Objects and Bring-Along Items:

Invite participants to bring along an object that represents something about
themselves—a hobby or interest, something about their work, or an interesting experience they have had.

In addition, encourage participants to bring quotes, short poems, or
Scripture verses related to this theme to share during worship and group
gatherings. This can be an engaging way to both learn more about one another and expand the repertoire of readings and songs during the retreat.

Finally, crowdsource pictures for the collage activity in the "Crafting Our Message" section. Invite participants to bring old magazines, greeting cards, and calendar pictures that can be cut up.

Leader's Tip:

Think about your own "bring-along" object. Consider an activity that you enjoy, or a place you have visited, or an interest that engages you which may not be widely known and which you are willing to talk about.

This retreat is based on the story of Esther found in chapters 1–8. Since the biblical account is too long to read out loud in its entirety during the retreat, creative ways must be found to convey the essence of the story and an understanding of the characters. Prior to the retreat, encourage participants to read the story, or even to watch a children's version on YouTube. Since not everyone will do this, some of the group gatherings focus on familiarizing participants with Esther's story.

Several printable children's versions of the story can be found online. These could be printed out and added to the book nook as an additional resource for participants.

Music Resources:

Music can be interspersed throughout the retreat at mealtimes, the beginning and conclusion of group gatherings, and during worship.

Hymns:

- "You Are The Seed (Sois La Semilla)" (tune: "Id Y Ensenad"). Spanish and English lyrics echo Jesus' Great Commandment, to share God's love while celebrating the gifts all God's children have to share.

- "Here I Am, Lord" (tune: "Here I Am") by Dan Shutte. Inspirational hymn that encourages us to offer ourselves to God's service.

- "This Little Light Of Mine" (tune: "This Little Light Of Mine"). Toe-tapping hymn urges us to share God's light.

Songs:

- "Beauty Queen, Song Of Esther" by Reev Robledo. A humorous yet poignant look at the challenges women face to be taken seriously. YouTube video sung by Micaela Pineda.

- "Born For This" by Mandisa. Powerful lyrics echo Esther's experience and remind listeners that "sometimes you gotta go, uninvited, sometimes you gotta speak when you don't have the floor."

- "Gloria" by U2. "Loosen my lips" so I can say what needs to be said. A fervent prayer.

- "I Am One Voice" by Don Eaton. The power of voices joining together. Easily learned with or without accompaniment.

- "People Have The Power" by Patti Smith. A powerful song encouraging us to discover our strength within.

- "Survivor" by Destiny's Child. Despite adversity and doubters, survival and never giving up are themes that inspire.

Creating the Atmosphere—Preparing Your Retreat Space:

- Display the retreat schedule in several places so it is easily seen by participants.

- Display posters with quotes that you have made.

- Display pictures of "Fearless Girl" statue and statue of Rosa Parks

Worship Area Suggestions:

When creating an altar, these items might be included:
- Candle on top of a bushel basket (Matt 5:15)
- Megaphone, microphone, or loudspeaker
- A broken chain
- The word "silence" with a line drawn through it

Activities and Discussion Questions for Group Gatherings:

These gatherings can be used in any order, depending on the needs of the group and time constraints.

Group Gathering: Exploring the characters in the book of Esther.

Background:

The five main characters from the book of Esther display their values (or lack of them) through their words and actions. This activity introduces these characters to participants.

Materials:

- Character introductions
- Bible for each small group, bookmarked at Esther
- Worksheet with questions for each small group

Activity:

Set up a station for each of the five characters. Each station has character introductions which include the following:

- Sign with character's name
- Introductory script
- Bible

Divide into small groups (three to four people).
Tell the groups:

> We will be meeting the characters from the story of Esther. There are five characters, one at each station. Designate a volunteer to read the character introduction out loud to your group. If your group would like more information about the character, you can look up the passage in the Bible.
>
> After your group has heard the introduction, one person should act as scribe. The scribe will record the group's responses on their worksheet.

WORKSHEET (THESE QUESTIONS ARE TO BE ANSWERED FOR EACH OF THE FIVE CHARACTERS).

1. What is your impression of this character? Write some words to describe this character.

2. Does this character remind you of any present-day or historical figure?

3. Write any questions or comments you may have.

Assign each group to a station. Monitor the groups to ensure they are advancing to the next station.

When the small groups have visited all five stations, re-assemble the group. Discuss each character using the worksheet questions and the questions below.

ADDITIONAL QUESTIONS:

- Which character did you like the most? Why?
- Which figure do you admire?

CHARACTER INTRODUCTIONS, BOOK OF ESTHER:

- I am Vashti. I was the first wife of King Xerxes. Although none of my words were ever recorded in the Bible, my actions spoke loudly. I did not wish to be paraded in front of a group of drunken men, so I refused the king's command to appear before him (1:12). I was true to myself, but my actions had consequences. Ultimately, I was silenced by a powerful man. The king took away my title and position. I was banished from the kingdom. I left the country and was never heard from again.

- I am King Xerxes. I am rich. I am powerful. My word is law. No one dares to question me. Critical thinking and asking questions are not my strong suit. When my advisors told me that the disobedience of my first wife Vashti could become a threat to the peace in our country, I believed them (1:18). When they recommended that she be banned from the country so that other women would not follow her rebellious example, I agreed with them (1:19). When my advisor Haman recommended that the Jewish people be killed because he found them to be disrespectful and arrogant, I took him at his word (3:8–11). Thank God, I had the good sense to marry Esther!

- I am Haman, the king's advisor. I like power. I yearn for wealth. I crave recognition and I demand that everyone bows down to me. When I am denied what I want, I am ruthless with my punishment (3:6). I rule by fear.

- I am Mordecai, Esther's uncle. It was my joy to raise my niece into the strong, gifted young woman she has become. I rejoice that she is now queen of our land. I believe that she is the right person at the right time. I trust that God can use her strength and faithfulness. I am a man of principle and deep faith. When I discovered a plot to assassinate the king, I did not hesitate to speak up (2:22). The traitors were captured and punished. Although I am proud of my Jewish faith, I advised Esther not to reveal her Jewish identity (2:20) so her safety would be ensured. But my faith compelled me to take a public stand and refuse to bow down to that slimy advisor, Haman (3:2). Only God is worthy of such honor. My actions made Haman angry, and now he wants to kill all of the Jews (3:6). I am devastated. I urge my niece Esther to risk her own life and approach the king to ask for mercy. I tell her, "Who knows? Perhaps you have come to royal dignity for just such a time as this" (4:14).

- I am Esther. Who could have imagined that I would ever be queen? I won the king's favor (2:17) and suddenly here I am, surrounded by wealth and power. And yet I do not always have power of my own.

Like anyone else, I can be killed if I enter the king's court without an invitation. Yet I know I must speak up in order to save my people from destruction. I ask my uncle Mordecai to have all the people pray for me to have wisdom and courage (4:15–16). I use my wits and power of persuasion to catch the king's attention and compel him to listen to my plea, which saves the Jewish people (8:5).

Group Gathering: Overview of Esther

Background:

This gathering helps participants become familiar with the story of Esther. By placing the Event Cards in the correct order, they will be able to briefly re-tell highlights from the biblical story.

Materials:

- Pack of seventeen Event Cards for each small group
- Bible for each small group; a Bible with section headings will be most helpful.

Activity:

Divide into small groups (two to four people). Provide each group with a Bible and a set of Event Cards.

Explain to the group:

> The story of Esther is action-packed. Each small group will learn about the story by placing the Event Cards in the correct order. If you are not sure about the order of the events, you can skim the first seven chapters of the book of Esther.
>
> Each Event Card describes one event. Place the Event Cards in order to tell the story of Esther.

Allow plenty of time (twenty to thirty minutes) to place event cards in order. When the groups have completed the exercise, invite one group to read their cards. If another group disagrees with the sequence, take the time to refer to the biblical story. Read through each card and discuss any questions.

Engage the group in conversation with these questions:

REFLECTION QUESTIONS:

- Do you have any questions about the story?
- What surprises you about the story?
- Do any of these events teach anything or contain wisdom for today?

The event cards can be taped down so participants can refer to the story throughout the retreat.

Group Gathering: Listening Exercise

Background:

Both Vashti and Esther conveyed important messages in different ways. Each of them took a risk to express themselves. The king listened to both women, but he responded in very different ways.

In this exercise, participants will have the opportunity to both speak and listen. It is important to be able to express ourselves. It is equally important to listen carefully; being a good listener is a valuable gift to offer.

Materials:

- Reflection questions
- Stopwatch or timer

Activity:

Divide the participants into pairs; if there are an odd number of participants, the leader can be part of a pair.

Explain to the group:

> Vashti conveyed her opinion not by speaking, but by refusing to obey the king's order. Esther's ability to speak up and challenge Haman saved the lives of the Jewish people. We will experience the importance of both speaking and listening.
>
> I will ask a question. In your pair, one person will speak and the other person will listen for ninety seconds. The listener is not allowed to make comments, ask questions, or interrupt. When time is up, roles will be reversed; the listener will now speak without interruption.
>
> We will do this exercise with three questions.

Invite the pairs to sit facing each other. They may adjust their chairs so they can hear one another. Ask each pair to decide who will speak first.

Once they are comfortable and have decided on their roles, read the first question. Set a timer for ninety seconds. When the time is up, invite the pair to reverse roles so the speaker now will become the listener.

Each pair will answer/listen to these questions:

REFLECTION QUESTIONS:

- What is an experience that brought you great joy?
- What advice would you give your younger self?
- Who is someone who has taught you important lessons?

Bring the group together and invite them to reflect on the experience with these questions:

DISCUSSION QUESTIONS:

- Was it easier to be the speaker or the listener?
- Did you enjoy one role more than another?
- Did you feel heard? Why or why not?
- Vashti expressed her opinion by refusing to obey the king's command. She was punished—he banished her from the kingdom. Does it make

it hard to speak up or express ourselves, knowing that someone else may not agree?

Group Gathering: Vashti and Esther

Background:

This activity explores courage. Participants will explore the courage of the biblical women Esther and Vashti, as well as other examples to determine what might encourage us to discover our voice.

Materials:

- Song: "Born for This"
- "Born For This" lyrics for each participant
- Song: "Here I Am, Lord"
- Picture of "Fearless Girl" statue
- Picture of Rosa Parks statue
- Newsprint divided in two columns labeled "Vashti" and "Esther"
- Newsprint entitled, "What are the consequences of speaking up?" Make three columns with the headings "Intended," "Unintended," and "Unexpected."
- Markers

Activity:

Tell the group that they will be exploring the courage that enables people to speak up or take a stand.

Point out the picture of the "Fearless Girl" statue. Encourage a discussion about the statue with these questions:

DISCUSSION QUESTIONS:

- What emotions does this statue elicit in you?
- If you could read the girl's mind, what is she thinking?
- Do you ever feel like that?
- If you could substitute the bull for a threatening object or person, what would it be?
- What gives the girl the courage to face the charging bull?

Point out the picture of the statue of Rosa Parks. Remind participants that Rosa Parks was an African-American woman who, in 1955, refused to give up her seat on a public bus to a white passenger. Her refusal to obey the segregation laws of the day sparked the Montgomery, Alabama bus boycott that lasted for more than a year.

Lead a discussion about the statue with these questions:

DISCUSSION QUESTIONS:

- Why were Rosa Parks' actions important?
- Rosa Parks is famous for what she did (remained seated on the bus) more than anything she said. What did her actions express?
- We know that her actions made some people very angry. What do you think gave her the courage to hold her ground?

Let the group know that they can keep thinking about these examples as they talk about the biblical characters Vashti and Esther.
Tell them:

> The song "Born For This" describes Esther discovering the nerve to speak an important truth.

Provide the participants with the lyrics for "Born For This." Play the song; engage the group in conversation with these questions:

- How does this song make you feel?

- How does it relate to the story of Esther?

- When is a time when we have to "go, uninvited," or "speak when we don't have the floor"?

- Do you think everyone was born with a specific task or calling? Could we have more than one? How do we discover what that might be?

Say to the group:

> Vashti and Esther both expressed themselves decisively, but in different ways. We have no record of Vashti's words, but her actions (refusing to obey the king's command to appear before him) sent a clear message of dissent. Esther expressed herself with actions (appearing before the king without an invitation, preparing lavish meals for the king and Haman) as well as courageous words (appealing to the king for mercy on behalf of her people, accusing Haman of treachery).
>
> We will explore the differences and similarities between the actions of Vashti and Esther. Point out to the group that speaking up (almost) always has consequences. Sometimes the consequences are unintended. Let's talk about some people whose actions changed things.

Invite a volunteer to record the responses on the Vashti/Esther labeled newsprint. Ask the group to consider the actions of Vashti and Esther and to list as many consequences as possible. Expand the discussion by encouraging the group to consider the results following the actions of Rosa Parks and other brave individuals who took a stand.

The song "Here I Am, Lord" can be played or sung to conclude this gathering.

Group Gathering: Discovering Our Voice

Background:

Vashti and Esther were both queens who make a significant impact in very different ways. Their courage can inspire our faithful response to challenging situations.

Materials:

- Pens
- Copy of discussion questions for each person

Activity:

Say to the group:

> Both Vashti and Esther had to respond to circumstances that were not of their making. Think about your own lives and situations as you answer the questions. You can write as much as you would like. You will share only what you choose with the group.

Provide participants with the discussion questions and invite them to write responses individually.

DISCUSSION QUESTIONS:

1. A time I spoke up was . . .
2. What is something I would like to speak up about now?
3. I hesitate to speak up because . . .
4. Who encourages me to speak? Who is my Mordecai? Or, who is someone who encourages me to speak?
5. Do you have a role model for someone who speaks up?
6. Is part of "speaking up" asking for help? Are you able to do that?

When participants have written their responses, divide them into small groups (three to five people) to share their responses.

Group Gathering: Identifying our Gifts

Background:

Esther, Vashti, and Mordecai used a variety of gifts and talents for the good of those around them. Esther demonstrates courage when she speaks truth to power, Vashti sets an example of dignity by refusing the king's drunken request, and Mordecai lives his faith by thwarting the king's enemies and refusing to humble himself before anyone except God.

Materials:

- Paper
- Pens
- "Identifying our gifts" worksheet

Activity:

After learning about Esther's inspiring story, it is time for participants to explore their own gifts.

Tell the group:

> Vashti, Esther, and Mordecai all used gifts and talents that they had to make a difference. Now it is time for each one of us to consider what gifts and strengths we have. Because all of us are created in the image of God and filled with God's Spirit, we know that everyone has gifts, talents and strengths.
>
> Think about your own gifts. These do not have to be dramatic characteristics. These are practical and spiritual attributes that you can use for God in big and small ways. Your gifts impact your family and friends.
>
> Please fill out the "Identifying Our Gifts" worksheet.

Provide each participant with a worksheet titled, "Identifying Our Gifts."

- My name is _____.
- Some of my gifts are (list at least five) _____.
- A gift I consider most important is _____.
- I use it by _____.
- The impact of my gift on others is _____.

In groups of three, invite the participants to share their reflections and talk about their own gifts. When everyone has had a chance to share, say to the group:

> The next step is to identify gifts in one another. Often other people value an attribute in us that we may not recognize or appreciate. In the same way that Mordecai encouraged Esther to realize the gifts that she possessed, it can be very powerful to hear others celebrate our gifts.

Invite the participants to tell one another about the gifts they recognize in each other. These gifts should be added to the list on each person's worksheet.

When the small groups have finished their conversation, bring the group together to discuss the experience of discovering our gifts.

Crafting Our Message: Creating a Message Collage

Purpose:

To create a personal message of expression as an inspiring reminder of the retreat's theme.

Materials:

- Magazines, calendar pages, greeting cards, catalogs
- Scissors
- Glue
- Posterboard cut into shapes about six inches wide. Shapes can include a rectangle, circle, triangle, star, or oval.

Directions:

Invite participants to think about the themes of speaking up and sharing our gifts. Tell the group:

> What inspirational message would you like to share—either with yourself or with someone else? It might be a message of encouragement for yourself, like "You can do this!", or it might be a message that you would like to share with the world (or some part of it), like "I will speak this truth."

Invite them to use the available materials to create an image with words and/or pictures to depict that message. Depending on time, participants may choose to create one message or more.

When participants have completed the craft, encourage them to share their messages with the group. These messages may be displayed and/or shared during worship.

Additional Craft Resources (for those who complete the craft early and are looking for further ideas):

- Adult coloring sheets (can be obtained free online)
- Colored pencils
- Pre-stamped postcards and pens (to be mailed by leader six to eight weeks after the retreat). Participants can write themselves a short note highlighting meaningful moments or quotes from the retreat.

Worship Resources:

These are themed resources to go with this particular retreat. Additional resources are available in the Appendix.

Litanies:

> Leader: Astonishing God, you fill us with your Spirit and your remarkable gifts.
>
> People: Open our minds that we may recognize the gifts and power within us and others.
>
> Leader: For the mosaic of our lives, patterns of people, and experiences that enrich us, we give you thanks.
>
> People: For bringing all these different people, opinions, and backgrounds together to form your church, we give you thanks.
>
> Leader: For calling us the Body of Christ, consisting of endless varieties of gifts and talents, we give you thanks.
>
> People: Creator and creative God, open us to your spirit and bring us together to form a vision of your new life and hope.

> Leader: Miraculous God, we come before you with thanksgiving and praise.
>
> People: Fill us with courage and wisdom in challenging moments.
>
> Leader: In the midst of turmoil, war, and strife, we ask for your guidance and strength.
>
> People: Fill us with courage to conquer our fears and wisdom to recognize the needs all around us.
>
> Leader: Where we can make a difference, let us act. When we can add encouragement, let us speak.
>
> People: Fill us with courage to say yes to you.

Unison prayers:

All around us, Lord, is need. We are overwhelmed at the global report of wars, poverty, unrest, racial injustice, and hunger. We turn off the news because we do not know what to do and become convinced that the problems are too great for us to tackle. Grant us wisdom and courage so that we may act when we can, speak up when we are able, and reach out to those in need. You have called us for such a time as this. Open our eyes that we may recognize opportunities to share your Good News of hope every day and everywhere. Amen.

> May I be inspired by biblical women filled with your courage and spirit:
> Like Vashti, may my actions speak louder than words.
> Like Esther, may I have the courage to speak truth to power.
> Like Mary, may I listen for your voice and trust in your word.
> Like Miriam, may I dance my joy and proclaim your hope.
> I name women from history and from today who let their voices be heard:
> Like Rosa, may I refuse to be moved or ignored.
> Like Maya, may I speak words of truth and encouragement.
> Like _____, may I _____ (allow time for individual responses).
> Filled with your gifts and your Spirit, loving God, may I share your vision
>   and hope. Amen.

Event Cards: The Story of Esther

These cards are used in Group Gathering: Overview of Esther.

Write each event on an index card or slip of paper. Provide each small group with a complete set of seventeen index cards. Instruct each group to place the facts in order so that they can retell Esther's story.

Note: the king is named Ahasuerus in some translations and Xerxes in others; I have chosen to use the name Xerxes throughout.

Event Cards:

- King Xerxes has a party that lasts for seven days.
- King Xerxes orders Queen Vashti to come before him and his friends to "show the peoples and the officials her beauty." Queen Vashti says no.
- The king is furious that Queen Vashti refused him. He orders her to be banished from the kingdom.
- Queen Vashti is gone. King Xerxes searches for a new queen.

- Many women were brought before the king, but he loved Esther and chose her to be his new queen. Esther does not tell the king she is Jewish.

- Unbeknownst to King Xerxes, Esther's uncle Mordecai prevented a plot to kill the king. The traitors were hanged, and the incident was recorded in the history books of the country.

- The king's evil advisor, Haman, wished to be treated with great honor. He demanded that everyone bow down before him when he passed by.

- Mordecai refused to bow to Haman because he would humble himself only to God.

- Haman was furious at Mordecai for his perceived lack of respect. When Haman discovered that Mordecai was Jewish, Haman asked the king to kill all the Jews in the country. The king issued a death decree to be fulfilled in a few days.

- Mordecai asked Esther to appeal to King Xerxes in order to save the Jewish people from death. Esther knew that she could be killed for approaching the king without an invitation, but she agreed to try.

- Queen Esther enters the court. She invites the king and Haman to a banquet.

- Banquet #1. Everyone has a good time! Esther invites the king and Haman to a second banquet.

- After the first banquet, Haman continues to be angry about Mordecai's continued refusal to honor him. Haman orders gallows to be built so Mordecai can be hanged.

- Before the second banquet, the king discovers that Mordecai saved him from traitors. He decides to honor Mordecai with riches and beautiful robes, much to the dismay of Haman.

- Banquet #2. The king is so pleased with Esther, he promises her anything—even half his kingdom! Esther asks for the freedom and safety of the Jewish people.

- The king asks who ordered the Jewish people to be killed. Esther answers, "A foe and enemy, this wicked Haman!" (Esther 7:5).

- Haman is hanged on the gallows he had built to kill Mordecai. Mordecai becomes the king's advisor. The Jewish people are saved. Esther is beloved throughout the land.

Chapter 5

Hope and Transformation

Discovering the Hidden Potential in Everyone

About This Theme:

Hope. It is the beacon we cling to when we wander in the darkness. It is the nourishment needed by a parched, weary soul. This retreat celebrates God's faithfulness in times of distress and God's refusal to abandon us, even when we drift away.

The legitimate concerns and real fears of people cannot be trivialized. Instead of offering the false claim that "everything will be just fine" (while ignoring daunting worries), the hope of the gospel is rooted in God's promise to journey with us on even the toughest roads. The resulting "transformation" may not be a miraculous alteration of our circumstances; instead, it may be a change within ourselves as we realize that, with God's help, we have the tools necessary to move forward.

This retreat offers biblical accounts of people who have discovered God's enduring presence while facing great challenges. God's people experience loss and desolation, cry out to God, and then hear God's promise to be with them in surprising and unexpected ways. The (re)discovery of God's presence in our lives can be a powerful transformational experience.

Scripture Focus:

- Isaiah 43:19–21
- Lamentations 3:21–28
- Ezekiel 11:19–20
- Mark 4:30–32

"Quotable":

- God said, "I establish my covenant with you" (Gen 8:8).
- "Do not be afraid; do not be discouraged. Be strong and courageous" (Josh 10:25).
- "They shall be my people, and I will be their God" (Ezek 11:20).
- "I am about to do a new thing . . . I give water in the wilderness" (Isa 43:19–20).
- "This I call to mind and therefore I have hope; the steadfast love of the Lord never ceases" (Lam 3:22).
- "If you wish to know the divine, feel the wind on your face and the warm sun on your hand."—Buddha
- "All shall be well, and all shall be well, and all manner of thing shall be well . . . for there is a Force of love moving through the universe that holds us fast and will never let us go."—Julian of Norwich

Introductory Objects and Bring-Along Items:

Invite participants to bring an object that symbolizes hope for them. It's often best not to give too many detailed instructions about the "bring-along" item; encourage participants to ponder the invitation, use their imaginations, and respond as they choose.

In addition, encourage participants to bring quotes, short poems, or Scripture verses related to this theme to share during worship and group gatherings. This can be an engaging way to both learn more about one another and expand the repertoire of readings and songs during the retreat.

Flexibility will be the key in responding to these songs or readings; a participant may be inspired to share in response to the current conversation. Whenever possible, the leader should encourage this spontaneity which often results in a powerful or meaningful insight.

Leader's Tip:

Take time to think about times when you have experienced hope and transformation in your own life. It is not necessary for you to talk about your personal experiences, but reflecting on moments when you have experienced hope breaking into a challenging situation will help prepare you for this theme.

Emily Dickinson's poem, "Hope is the thing with feathers," is a lovely reading for this theme.

Music Resources:

Music can be interspersed throughout the retreat at mealtimes, the beginning and conclusion of group gatherings, and during worship.

Mustard seed shakers can be created to provide a tangible reminder of Jesus' parable (Mark 4:30–32) and a fun accompaniment to the music. Add mustard seeds (available by the pound online) to baby food jars, film canisters, or another small container with a lid. This can be a tangible reminder of Jesus' parable.

Hymns:

- "Amazing Grace" (tune: "New Britain"). This hymn is by definition a song about hope and transformation. Because it is familiar to many people, you may wish to offer a variety of renditions and tempos. The transformational story of the hymn's author, John Newton, is inspiring.
- "In The Bulb There Is A Flower" (tune: "Promise"). Author Natalie Sleeth penned these beautiful lyrics as her husband was critically ill. The hymn was played at his funeral as a reminder that God's presence is sometimes hidden, but always promised. Even as circumstances change, hope emerges in new forms.

- "Great Is Your Faithfulness" (tune: "Faithfulness"). Inspired by Lamentations 3:22–23, this beautiful hymn praises God for faithful, dependable love.

Songs:

- "Build A Bridge" by Mavis Staples. With a compelling rhythm, Mavis Staples declares she will overcome any obstacle to "come right over to you."
- "Change My Heart O God" by Vineyard. Inspired by Jeremiah 18:1–6, this song encourages us to place ourselves trustingly in God's hands.
- "Go Light Your World" by Chris Rice. Each of us has God's light within us that we are encouraged to share.
- "Grace" by Jars of Clay. The upbeat tempo delivers a powerful message about God's faithfulness, even when we are reluctant to change.
- "Imagine" by John Lennon. This classic defines the word "hope" by imagining a world where barriers fall and all people get along.
- "Rise Up" by Andra Day. This beautiful song describes moments when we are "broken down and tired," but must still find a way to "rise up."
- "We Shall Overcome." Civil rights era anthem of motivation and hope.
- "You Are The Potter, I Am The Clay." There is a beautiful version by Judy Moore available on YouTube.

Creating the Atmosphere—Preparing Your Retreat Space:

- Display the schedule for your retreat in several places so it is easily seen by participants.
- Display posters with quotes that you have made.
- Display posters with images of plants and trees that you have made.
- Make two to three posters using images from Google (or a similar search engine). Find images of trees or plants growing in unlikely places (for example, a flower growing through a sidewalk crack or a tree reaching out roots to find water). Place the image at the top of a

page (it can simply be a 11 x 17 sheet of paper) so that there is room for participants to write captions for the pictures underneath the picture.

Worship Area Suggestions:

When creating your worship area, you might include these items:

- Symbols of new life and resurrection: plant, flower, flower bulb, egg, seeds, butterflies
- Fabric with flower or butterfly motif
- A candle or electric votive

Activities and Discussion Questions for Group Gatherings:

These gatherings can be used in any order, depending on the needs of the group and time constraints.

Group Gathering: The Power of a Mustard Seed

Background:

Jesus' parable of the mustard seed is one example of God offering new life in unlikely places. This very short story offers wisdom about great results that can develop from even the smallest efforts. Participants will discover the new life that emerges from transformational growth.

Materials:

- Song: "Go Light your World"
- Mark 4:30–32
- Pictures of mustard seed and mustard plants
- Paper and pens for each participant
- There are several brief videos of the mustard seed parable on YouTube that can provide an enjoyable introduction to this story.

Activity:

Read the parable of the mustard seed (Mark 4:30–32) to the group. It is very short, so take the time to read it twice. Show the group the pictures of the mustard seed and the mustard plant; encourage them to notice the difference in size between the two. Ask them to name other examples from nature of a small seed producing a large plant (a flower emerging from a bulb, a tall pine tree spring forth from pine cone seeds, and so on).

Tell the group:

> Hope is like that tiny seed that grows a mustard plant. This Good News can lift our hearts and offer us new life in times of sadness or need. We can be encouraged by remembering that even our small efforts can have a big impact. Invite them to think of people in the news who inspire hope or display a hopeful attitude.

Ask the group what challenge(s) each of those people face. Ask a volunteer to record these answers on a piece of newsprint labeled "People of Hope." Once a list is developed, ask the group if these people have anything in common (they may not, but it is interesting to explore).

The song "Go Light Your World" celebrates the power of sharing hope; hope can light and change the world. Play the song for the group and ask them how the people they have listed have shared their light with the world, and what difference that has made.

Having named public examples of hope, the participants can consider where they encounter hope in their own lives. Provide participants with paper and pens.

Tell the group:

> Now we can think about someone we know (or knew) who taught us about hope. Think about those who planted seeds of hope and whose light has gone out to change the world. Write down their names and a little bit about each person.

Divide into groups of three to five people. Invite everyone to talk about the people they listed. Let the groups know how much time they have so that each person has a chance to share their stories.

During a worship time, you may want to use one of the litanies of hope to give thanks for these people who have touched our lives and taught us about hope (see "Worship Resources" in this chapter). Participants can be invited to name some of these people of hope as part of a litany or prayer.

Group Gathering: God Does a New Thing

Background:

As participants listen to the voice of the prophets speaking to people who have suffered great loss, they can hear God's voice of hope spoken in times of need.

Materials:

- Isaiah 43:19–21 in several translations
- Ezekiel 11:19–20
- Reflection questions for each participant
- Pens
- Songs: "Build a Bridge," "Amazing Grace," or another song of your choice

Activity:

Let the group know they will be hearing Scriptures that depict God providing hope to the people.

Tell the group about the prophets Ezekiel and Isaiah, who share glimpses of God's hope with those who are discouraged or weary. After a long period of feeling cut off from God, the prophets announce that God's people will experience God in a new way. The people have not, in fact, been abandoned by God; the prophets describe how God's love and compassion will be demonstrated.

Isaiah describes God making a new path in the crowded, overwhelming wilderness and creating much-needed rivers in the dry, parched desert. He describes a period of transformation that will result in new life.

Ezekiel shares God's words of hope. Through the prophet, God says that the "heart of stone" currently found in God's people will be removed and will be replaced by a new, loving, receptive spirit.

Ask a volunteer to read Isaiah 43:19–21 to the group. If possible, use more than one translation (translations such as the Message or the Voice offer a very different feel).

Ask another volunteer to read Ezekiel 11:19–20 out loud.

Engage the group in conversation by asking:

REFLECTION QUESTIONS:

- Isaiah describes life's challenging moments as living in a wilderness or experiencing a dry time. What are examples of "dry" or challenging times in life?

- What kind of words or phrases do we use to describe those tough times?

Provide each participant with the reflection questions below, as well as copies of the Scriptures they just heard. Invite the participants to read the questions and take some time (about fifteen to twenty minutes) to thoughtfully record their answers individually in silence:

REFLECTION QUESTIONS:

1. Do you find yourself in a wilderness or in a dry place in your life right now? Describe what that is like for you. Or, do you know someone who is experiencing a challenging time right now? What is that like for them?

2. Have you ever felt like you had a hard heart that was unable to care, or a bruised heart that had been hurt by others? Is it possible for those damaged hearts to receive a new or healing spirit?

3. What new thing do you need? What new direction or change are you looking for?

When participants have answered these questions, take the time to listen to a song of hope such as "Build a Bridge" or "Amazing Grace." Ask participants what messages of hope they hear.

Read the Isaiah passage once more. Divide into smaller groups (three to five people) and invite them to talk about their responses. Allow at least thirty minutes for conversation; encourage them to be mindful of the time so everyone has an opportunity to share.

When the time is complete, bring the group back together. Ask if any of the groups would like to share their reflections, or if there were any common themes that people discovered in their stories. (Allow at least fifteen minutes for this large group reflection).

Group Gathering: Bulbs—Hidden Potential

Background:

Flower bulbs provide a wonderful metaphor for hidden potential. The source of hope and new life is not always visible, but is nonetheless present. There is a "time for every season" (Ecclesiastes 3:1); sometimes we have to wait for hope and new life to be apparent.

Materials:

- Song: "In The Bulb There Is A Flower"
- Lyrics to "In The Bulb There Is A Flower" for each participant
- Pictures of tulips, daffodils, crocuses, and other plants that grow from bulbs
- Discussion questions for each participant
- Pens

Activity:

Play the hymn "In The Bulb There Is A Flower." Being mindful of copyright laws (which usually grant permission to copy lyrics with proper attribution to be used by small groups), provide the lyrics for participants to read along.

Show the group pictures of flowers that have emerged from bulbs. Encourage participants to discuss what they know about bulbs, flowers, and the dormant stage that is necessary in order for the bulb to grow into its intended beauty.

If the group is larger than ten participants, divide into smaller groups. Invite the groups to engage in conversation with the following questions:

PART 1 REFLECTION QUESTIONS:

1. How would you describe yourself today? Bulb? Flower? Somewhere in between?

2. When have you experienced a time of renewal or rebirth?

3. Talk about a time when you overcame an obstacle or challenge

4. What did you learn from that? How did you grow?

Invite the groups back together to reflect on their conversation.

Tell the group it is time to celebrate the hope God provides to each of us. Whether we are experiencing a time of dormancy or bursting forth in full bloom, God surrounds us with care and strength.

Play a song like "Grace," "Rise Up," or another that is uplifting.

Provide each participant with the Part 2 reflection questions. Allow them ten to fifteen minutes to answer these questions on their own before forming small groups for discussion.

PART 2 REFLECTION QUESTIONS:

1. How do past experiences of renewal (times when you have overcome obstacles) help you with whatever challenge you are facing today?

2. What is something in you or about your situation that "God alone can see"?

3. What is giving you a seed of hope right now?

4. Who is helping you see/experience hope?

When the groups have completed their conversations, bring the whole group back together. If possible, sing a song such as "Amazing Grace" or "Great Is Your Faithfulness" together.

Group Gathering: God Is the Potter, We Are the Clay

Background:

There may be times when we yearn for something new, but practically speaking are unable to find our way forward. There are times when the mistakes we have made or challenges that we face seem too great to overcome. The notion that God can gently mold us into God's image can provide hope; God sees potential in us even when we cannot.

Materials:

- Discussion questions for each participant
- Newsprint
- Markers
- Tape
- Song: "Change My Heart O God"

Activity:

Tell the group that many Scripture verses emphasize putting away the old and embracing the new. Some examples are:

- Lamentations tells us that God's mercies are "new every morning" (3:23).
- Isaiah announces that God is "about to do a new thing" (43:19).
- After the flood, God urges Noah to "go forth" into the new land (Gen 8:15).
- John rejoices that God will make "all things new" (Rev 21:5).

The song "Change My Heart, O God" is a prayer asking God to change and mold our hearts so we are better able to serve God.

Play the song. Tell the group that wanting something "new" doesn't have to mean that the "old" is bad. It may simply indicate that we are open to different experiences and prepared to imagine a different way to encounter familiar and new experiences. Remind them that we worship the Creator of the universe, made with all of its diversity and variations. This God of new life and infinite possibilities can even lead us into new understandings of routine or unchangeable circumstances. Sometimes it is not our situation that is transformed; rather, it can be our attitude or our outlook that shifts and allows us to recognize God in that place.

Divide the participants into groups of three people. Tell them to read over the questions silently before discussing them in their small groups.

REFLECTION QUESTIONS:

1. What is an attitude/habit/lifestyle that you would like to put behind you?

2. What is the new heart, new spirit that you long for? What would you ask God for?

3. What new direction do you want to take?

4. What is something new that you could embrace?

When the small groups have completed their discussion, bring the group back together. Ask them what similarities and differences they discovered in their responses.

Engage the group in conversation with the following questions as a volunteer records their answers:

DISCUSSION QUESTIONS:

1. Name a situation in the world where "something new" is needed. Think about families, communities, congregations, and events around the world. Remembering that God's compassion far exceeds ours can inspire us to identify needs near and far.

2. Create a list of situations/circumstances/people that need God's "new heart" (Ezek 11:19). These can be lifted up in prayer during worship.

Group Gathering: Molded in God's Image

Background:

The prophet Jeremiah provides a beautiful image of God as a potter. Knowing that we are safe in God's hands, we can allow ourselves to be gently molded by God so we may serve God.

Materials:

- Song: "You Are The Potter, I Am The Clay"
- Jeremiah 18:1–6
- Small amounts of modeling clay for each participant

Activity:

Provide participants with small amounts of modeling clay. Encourage them to hold the clay as a volunteer reads Jeremiah 18:1–6.

Tell the participants:

> The prophet Jeremiah describes each of us as a piece of clay being shaped by God's loving hands. When something isn't quite right or the clay takes on the wrong shape, the potter simply re-molds the clay. The clay isn't discarded, but is given the opportunity to take on a new form.

Play the song: "You Are The Potter, I Am The Clay."

Let the participants knows that they have ten to fifteen minutes to create a symbol of new life or change with their piece of clay. This can be a simple symbol that is meaningful to them in their quest for transformation with God's help.

Bring the whole group together and encourage them to briefly share their symbols. These may be added to the worship area, if desired.

Crafting Our Message: Message Magnets

Purpose:

Create small magnets with a word or image to remind participants of hope and transformation.

Materials:

- Newsprint
- Markers
- Used magazines, brochures, catalogs
- Scissors
- Permanent craft adhesive (E6000 works well; available at craft stores or online)
- Small flat clear marbles (often used in vases). These can be found in a craft store or ordered online. Enough for five to eight marbles per person.
- Small magnets that will fit on the flat clear marbles
- Small boxes to hold the completed magnets (optional, but it provides a neat way to transport the magnets home). Small cardboard, tin, or wooden boxes can be purchased at a craft store.

Directions:

Tell the participants:

> We will be creating messages on magnets that reflect the themes of hope and transformation. The magnets can be placed in areas at home, office, or in the car to remind us of God's enduring promise of presence.

Encourage them to take a few moments to think of images or words that relate to the conversations and discussions that have taken place. Invite participants to call out words or phrases that reflect the retreat's theme. These can be written on newsprint to help participants in their search.

Invite participants to look through magazines and catalogs to find images and words that appeal to them. Since the magnets are relatively small, they should focus on one image or word at a time. Encourage them to take the time to find several images/words and to cut them out to the size that will fit on the base of the clear marble.

The magnets will be assembled in this order:

1. Put a tiny drop of glue on the selected image

2. Place this on the flat marble base so that the image is visible through the glass

3. Put a small drop of glue on the magnet and gently press it onto the paper already on the base.

Once the glue has dried, place magnets in a box. You may wish to invite participants to share one or two of their images or words during a group gathering or worship time.

Additional Craft Resources (for those who complete the craft early and are looking for further ideas):

- Adult coloring sheets (can be obtained free online)
- Colored pencils
- Pre-stamped postcards and pens (to be mailed by leader six to eigh weeks after the retreat). Participants can write themselves a short note highlighting meaningful moments or quotes from the retreat.

Worship Resources:

These are themed resources to go with this particular retreat. Additional resources are available in the Appendix.

Litanies of Hope

Note: these two litanies make use of water-activated LED candles (such as Lumizu Water-Activated LED Floating Candles) by placing them into a clear bowl of water. The illuminated candles symbolize glimmers of hope and the promise of God's light and presence with us always.

Leader: In the midst of despair, God provides hope and an assurance that we are not alone.

People: We give thanks for God's messengers, who have embodied God's love for us.

Leader: God's steadfast love can appear in our lives, sometimes in very unlikely ways.

People: Today we give thanks for those light-bearers, those people who have broken into our shadows with the light of God's love.

Leader: Let us name those heralds of Good News and hope:

Invite participants to name someone who has offered them hope or encouragement. As the name is said, the participant can place the water-activated candle into the basin of water.

Leader: God remembered Noah and spoke words of hope in the midst of a muddy, messy world shattered by flood.

People: God says to us, "I will make a covenant with you. A promise that can never be broken. A relationship that can never end."

Leader: God remembered Noah and offered a sign, a rainbow to light up the sky after the storm.

People: God says to us, "I will make a covenant with you. A promise that can never be broken. A relationship that can never end."

Leader: God remembers us, wherever we are, in whatever circumstances we find ourselves.

People: God says to us, "I will make a covenant with you. A promise that can never be broken. A relationship that can never end."

Leader: Today we give thanks that, even in the messiness of our own lives, God's light shines. Today we celebrate the covenant that God has made with each one of us.

Invite each participant to come forward and place the water-activated LED candle into the basin of water and say, "God's covenant is with me."

Chapter 6

Beyond the Dreamcoat
Living in Relationship

About This Theme:

Living in relationship with others can be a challenge! Parents, siblings, coworkers, colleagues, congregations, neighbors—each of us live within many webs of personalities and systems. Joseph and his complicated family offer valuable insights as we navigate the issues of our own lives and relationships.

This retreat encourages participants to reflect on their relationships with others as well as with God. As participants recall Joseph's tumultuous life, they will reflect on the ups and downs of human relationships and learn about God's faithfulness in their own lives.

Scripture Focus:

- Genesis 37
- Psalm 130

"Quotable":

- "Even though you intended to do harm to me, God intended it for good" (Gen 50:20).

- "Do not fear, for I have redeemed you; I have called you by name, you are mine" (Isa 43:1).

- "Give thanks to the God of heaven, for his steadfast love endures forever" (Ps 136:26).

- "This is my beloved" (Matt 3:17).

- "Never give up, for that is just the place and time that the tide will turn."—Harriet Beecher Stowe

Introductory Objects and Bring-Along Items:

Invite participants to bring a gift or present that they were given. It may have sentimental value only for them, but somehow this object let them know that they were valued or loved and continues to remind them of this truth.

In addition, encourage participants to bring quotes, short poems, or Scripture verses related to this theme to share during worship and group gatherings. This can be an engaging way to both learn more about one another and expand the repertoire of readings and songs during the retreat.

Leader's Tip:

It will be useful for this retreat to ensure that participants are familiar with the story of Joseph. While the entire story of Joseph spans fourteen chapters in Genesis, participants should be encouraged to read at least Genesis 37 prior to the retreat. Time should be taken during the retreat to review the story (using "Joseph's Story" in Group Gathering: Actions and Consequences) so participants will have a greater appreciation of Joseph's circumstances.

Music Resources:

Music can be interspersed throughout the retreat at mealtimes, the beginning and conclusion of group gatherings, and during worship.

Hymns:

- "God Is My Shepherd" (tune: "Brother James' Air"). One of many versions of Psalm 23, this hymn reflects quiet confidence in God's abiding presence.
- "God Is Working His Purpose Out" (tune: "Purpose"). A strong beat conveys the message of God's relentless work on behalf of God's people.
- "God's Eye Is On The Sparrow" (tune: "Sparrow"). Beautiful reassurance of God's loving concern.
- "Out Of The Depths" (tune: "Fennville"). A powerful song of forgiveness, healing and renewal with guitar chords make this a wonderful choice for group singing.

Songs:

- "Coat Of Many Colors" by Dolly Parton. Inspired by the Joseph story, a modern story of a multicolored coat.
- "God Delights In You" by Sovereign Grace. Despite what anyone else tells you, God delights in you.
- "Joseph And The Technicolor Dreamcoat" by Andrew Lloyd Webber, Tim Rice. Several songs from this Broadway musical help tell the story of Joseph and his brothers.
- "Joseph's Coat." Joseph is favored by his father and receives his multicolored coat.
- "Joseph's Dream." Joseph's vision of his future power and success.
- "Poor, Poor Joseph." Betrayed by his brothers, Joseph is sold into slavery.
- "Thy Word" by Amy Grant. Speaks of God's reassuring voice in times of fear and doubt.
- "We Shall Not Give Up The Fight." Inspiring South African freedom song.
- "Word Of God Speak" by Bart Millard and Pete Kipley. Encouragement to listen for God's voice.

Creating the Atmosphere—Preparing Your Retreat Space:

Fill the retreat space with positive messages about God's love and presence (for example: "Lo, I am with you always"; "God's not through with me yet"). This will provide a strong contrast to the negative messages pushed on Joseph by his brothers.

Worship Area Suggestions: When Creating Your Worship Area, Consider Including These Items:

- Multicolored scarves or fabric
- Butterflies
- Sign or wooden blocks reading "you are loved" or "beloved"

Activities and Discussion Questions for Group Gatherings:

These gatherings can be used in any order, depending on the needs of the group and time constraints.

Group Gathering: Actions and Consequences

Background:

Joseph's famous coat becomes a symbol of complex family relationships where mistakes are made and everyone gets hurt. Genesis 37 depicts Jacob treating his sons unequally. Joseph takes advantage of being his father's favorite, and that leads his brothers to uncaring and violent actions. This activity reveals the impact that a single gift can have on an entire family.

Materials:

- Readers' Theater: "Joseph's Story"
- Songs: "Joseph's Coat" and "Poor, Poor Joseph"
- Newsprint and markers
- Tape

Activity:

The story of Joseph's coat, or robe, dominates people's imagination. Often when people think about Joseph, they make the connection with his famous coat. Before you begin the activity, ask participants to list whatever they know—or think they know—about Joseph, his coat, and his family. List these words or phrases on newsprint.

Let the group know that they will learn about Joseph and his coat (and why this gift was so important to him and his brothers) by listening to a song from the musical "Joseph And The Technicolor Dreamcoat" by Andrew Lloyd Webber. Encourage them to listen particularly for the father's voice and the eleven brothers' reaction to the coat given to Joseph.

- Play the song "Joseph's Coat."
- Ask participants to name their impressions of the characters.
- Invite seven volunteers to read Joseph's story to the group, explaining that all seven people are speaking in the first person and relating Joseph's story.

Tell the group:

> There are complicated family dynamics going on in this story! No one behaved very well. Let's take some moments to describe where they went wrong. Let's consider three characters one at a time—there is Jacob (the father), Joseph, and the brothers (we'll think of them as a unit). Make a list of their characteristics and the mistakes they make.

Ask a volunteer to record the responses. Encourage the group to discuss how the words and actions of each character impacted and changed the lives of those in their family.

Engage the group in conversation with these questions:

REFLECTION QUESTIONS:

- Do you think parents often have a favorite child? Is it okay to express that?
- What could have prevented the anger of the brothers against Joseph?

- Is sibling rivalry a given in every family? Is that something parents should encourage or discourage?

- What could have prevented the anger of the brothers against Joseph?

- What kind of rivalries or competition occur in other situations—for example, in the workplace, church, community groups, or neighborhoods? How can we discourage cutthroat competition and instead foster cooperation?

The song "Poor, Poor Joseph" continues Joseph's story as he suffers the consequences of his brother's wrath.

Play that song and ask for participants' reactions.

Readers' Theater: Joseph's Story

This first-person account is inspired by Genesis 37. Although Joseph is the speaker throughout, invite several participants to read to remind listeners that this story belongs to everyone regardless of age or gender.

> Speaker 1: My name is Joseph. I am seventeen years old, the son of Jacob and Rachel. I have—get this!—ten older brothers and one sister, Dinah. Do you want to know the boys' names? Never mind—you'd never remember, and besides, I'm the main character in this story.
>
> My father has flocks and flocks of sheep. Lots of them. And they need to be watched and tended to. Sheep—they are not the brightest animal on the block. They need to be led to green pastures, they need help finding still waters, and they need to be protected from wild animals and even from sharp ledges and steep cliffs. They would walk right off a cliff if you weren't paying attention. It's a full-time job. Someone always has to be watching over them.
>
> Speaker 2: It's a good thing I have so many brothers! We take turns watching the sheep, but it still means long, hot days and even longer nights, in all kinds of weather. Being a shepherd is a full-time job. It is hard, thankless work.
>
> And I have to say—my brothers aren't always that good at it. Sometimes they get bored. Sometimes they fall asleep. Sometimes they are more interested in the village girls going to the well than the scraggly, wooly critters they are supposed to be watching.
>
> I let my father know that they weren't the most reliable guys on the planet.

Speaker 3: My father was an old man. I was one of the sons of his beloved wife, Rachel. I think I reminded him of her. I guess you could say I was his favorite son. You may think that parents are not supposed to have favorites, but sometimes it happens. He loved me more than any of his other children.

So, he gave me a wonderful gift. It was a beautiful long robe and—it had long sleeves! Some people have described it as a coat of many colors, but the shape of the coat was the important thing. A robe with long sleeves lets people know that the wearer is a man of worth and importance. You can't move fast in a long robe—you kind of glide across the ground like a dignified person. And the sleeves tell everyone that this person is not expected to work. A farmer doesn't wear long sleeves. A real shepherd always has short sleeves or no sleeves so he wouldn't get tangled up in the briars or get it covered with dirt.

I am now a man with a long robe and sleeves. I am a man of status.

Speaker 4: You can imagine what my brothers thought about that! My brothers were angry. You know the green-eyed monster? That's jealousy—and my brothers were filled with it. They hated me. They could hardly stand the sight of me.

Speaker 5: Things only got worse when I started having dreams. I dreamed that the sun, the moon, and eleven stars all bowed down to me. I knew it meant that someday I would have power over my brothers—and maybe even over my parents. When my brothers heard *that*, they hated me even more.

Speaker 6: Things happened fast after that. My brothers wanted to get rid of me. They were so angry with me that they couldn't see any value or worth in me. They forgot—or didn't care—that my father loved me. They just wanted me gone. So, when I went out to the field—the distant field, far from where we lived, and out of sight of anyone or anything—they planned to kill me. Granted, Reuben tried to speak up for me, but he was not willing to go against the rest. They were going to just toss me into a pit and tell my father that wild animals had eaten me up. But then—a slave trader happened to be passing by. Judah suggested that they get rid of me—and make money in the bargain. While they were discussing it, some Midianite travelers came along, saw me, sold me, and made the money themselves. I was gone when my brothers returned.

Speaker 7: They tore my beautiful robe off of me. They tossed me into a deep pit and then left me to slave traders. The traders took me away—away from my country, my home, and my family. My brothers didn't care. It was as if they were telling me I had no value or worth. They just sold me. Then they broke my father's heart by telling him I had died. Their words and their actions changed my life forever. It changed our family, too.

Group Gathering: Dealing with Bullies

Background:

Throughout the Joseph story, the characters tell lies and half-truths. When the father gives Joseph an extravagant gift, he hints (though never directly says) that the brothers have less value than Joseph.

The brothers' brutal actions tell Joseph he is not worthy of basic respect or dignity. The brothers compound their guilt by lying to their father when they report Joseph's death. These falsehoods shatter their relationships and have a devastating impact on their family.

Materials:

- Sheet entitled "God's lasting love" and containing the verses Deuteronomy 7:9; Psalm 86:15; and Psalm 136:26.
- Reflection Questions for each participant
- Pens

Activity:

Scripture tells us that we are known, named, and loved by God. The brothers told lies about Joseph—they made him feel as if he had no worth, that no one cared. They told each other lies to convince one another that their actions were justified. They told their father a lie and allowed him to dwell in sorrow. Lies can have powerful consequences.

Say to the group:

> Joseph's brothers were bullies. They banded together to harm Joseph with their words and actions. It might make us wonder why some people become bullies—what creates a bully?

Engage the group in conversation with these questions:

REFLECTION QUESTIONS:

- How do you think bullies are formed?
- How you ever experienced bullying?
- Although we typically think of bullying as a childhood issue, many people experience bullying or intimidation in the workplace or in their neighborhoods. Can you think of examples?

Being in the pit was supposed to be the end of Joseph's life and the end of his story. The pit is a frightening place to be. Joseph had been abandoned there by people who were supposed to love him, or at least care for him. He must have been heartbroken and scared.

At some point in our lives, we all experience a time in the "pit," a time of loneliness or discouragement. While we might wish our lives could be "pit-less," we know that isn't true. There are times when we sink in or get pushed into a pit.

Divide into small groups and invite participants to talk about the following questions:

REFLECTION QUESTIONS:

- What is it like in the pit?
- What emotions do we experience?
- What can help us when we are feeling alone or lonely?
- What makes us scared and what can break through that fear?
- Think about a time when you experience the "pit" but managed to come out of it. What made that possible?
- Bring the groups back together and ask them to share highlights of their discussion.

Say to the group:

> Ultimately, Joseph's story is one of resurrection. He was
> meant to die, but he was given a second chance at living. The
> brothers' goal was to destroy him, but God had other plans.

Tell the group that, instead of listening to the brothers' lies, we will listen to God's truth. Invite three volunteers to read Deuteronomy 7:9, Psalm 86:15, and Psalm 136:26.

Engage the group in conversation with these questions:

REFLECTION QUESTIONS:

- How are God's words different from those of the brothers?
- What does God promise?
- What does God say to God's people?

Group Gathering: Daring to Speak Up

Background:

Joseph's angry brothers plotted to kill him. However, Rueben pleaded, "Let us not take his life" (Gen 37:21); Reuben hoped he could rescue Joseph and return him to their father. He attempted to be a lone voice of reason in violent circumstances. Although he prevented Joseph from being killed, Rueben was silent when the slave traders paid twenty pieces of silver for Joseph and transported him to a life of bondage in a foreign land.

Materials:

- Newsprint
- Posterboard
- Markers
- Tape
- Song: "We Shall Not Give Up The Fight"

- Reflection questions

Activity:

Tell the group they will be considering times and places where our voices can make a difference.

Say to the group:

> Joseph's brother Reuben is an example of someone who made a difference by speaking up. At the same time, Reuben failed to say anything to prevent the violent plans of the slave traders. What Joseph needed was someone to speak up on his behalf in order to stop the injustice of being sold into slavery. No one did that.

The South African freedom song "We Shall Not Give Up The Fight" provided encouragement for those affected by the devastating system of apartheid. The inspiring lyrics remind listeners that their voices and actions can strengthen the struggle for justice.

Invite participants to listen to the song. Make two lists on newsprint: "Global or national circumstances" and "Personal or local circumstances." Invite participants to list local and global situations where our voices and energy are needed. Encourage them to consider circumstances where suffering or injustice exists; these may be divided into the two categories or broadened into additional descriptions. Encourage them to name situations from the news as well as circumstances closer to home.

Note to leader: Participants should be encouraged to only talk about examples that they are comfortable sharing. Everyone's personal history is different; some people have experienced more personal trauma and may choose not to discuss that. Remind participants that this is a safe space and they may choose how much to share.

Engage the group in conversation with the following questions:

REFLECTION QUESTIONS:

- What are some historical examples of times when people have remained silent in the face of evil or danger?

- Are any of the situations listed on newsprint similar to events in the past?

- What voice does each situation require? What needs to be said?

- What prevents us from speaking up? Have there been times when I have wanted to speak up, but then went along with the crowd?

Say to the group:

> The song "We Shall Not Give Up The Fight" provides encouragement to continue on in the struggle against oppression.

Divide into smaller groups (three to five people) and provide them with newsprint (or posterboard) and markers, so they can create posters with slogans of empowerment and encouragement. Participants should read over the list of situations compiled by the whole group. Direct them to create a poster that tells people how to respond to those circumstances of injustice or suffering. They can use slogans, words, or drawings to inspire people into action.

When the groups have completed their posters, they can share them with the entire group. The posters can be displayed or added to the worship center.

Group Gathering: Identifying and Confronting Lies

Background:

Society is filled with lies. The media tells us who and what are important. Hidden and overt messages tell us how we should look or act, what we should eat or wear, or what we need in order to have value.

Sometimes we say negative things to ourselves; we are often our own harshest critics. This activity encourages participants to examine those negative statements and celebrate God's loving truth.

Materials:

- Magazines
- Scissors
- Glue

- Paper
  - Markers
  - Posterboard
  - Scripture quotes: Psalm 103:12; Daniel 9:9; Hebrews 10:17; Romans 8:37–39
  - Song: "Thy Word," "Word of God Speak," or other song of your choice

Activity:

Engage the group in conversation by comparing the lies told by Joseph's brothers with the demeaning messages relayed by advertisers. Remind the group that, just as Joseph was told he was of no value, so we are told that we are lacking in material possessions, physical appearance, or ability.

Reflection Questions:

- What negative messages do we hear from advertisers?
- What do they want us to believe? Why?
- How are young people targeted by advertisers? What can be the consequences?

Divide into smaller groups to create a poster contrasting the words of media and the words of God. Provide each group with Scripture quotes emphasizing God's forgiveness and love. Tell the groups to divide the posterboard in half; one half will detail the falsehoods we hear, while the other half will speak God's truth. Encourage them to use the provided materials to create the poster. If the provided magazines do not offer the messages they are seeking, they may create their own with paper and markers.

When the groups have completed their posters, bring them together to discuss the negative and positive messages they listed. The posters may be displayed in the worship area.

Tell the group:

> It is not only others that send us negative messages. Sometimes we tell ourselves things that are not true; we can be very harsh critics of ourselves. Together we will state some of the negative messages that we tell ourselves and then counteract each one by saying, "But God says—each one of us is God's beloved child."

Encourage participants to call out negative statements that people say to themselves. After each statement, lead the group in the response, "But God says—we are God's beloved child."

Ask the group:

> What can we do to remember God's words and to keep this truth in front of us? How will we ignore the negative and focus on God's loving message for us?

Play the song "Thy Word" or another song to conclude this group gathering.

Group Gathering: Re-Writing the Message

Background:

Josephs' brothers embody a strong negative message of betrayal and lack of compassion. With their words and actions, they tell Joseph that he has little worth; they are willing to discard him with no regard for his well-being.

We live in a world that often delivers negative messages. God has a different message for us. This activity encourages participants to reflect God's words of love and create messages of motivation and support. By arranging and rearranging the provided words, participants can compose loving memos of compassion and encouragement.

Materials:

- Word list for each small group
- Pens

Activity:

Divide into small groups (two to four participants). Tell them:

> So often we hear negative messages from the media or advertising. Everyone seems to want to tell us what is wrong with us and what we are lacking. God's message for us is exactly the opposite. God regards us as God's beloved children. Today we are going to imagine the messages that God might have for us.

Give each group a word list. Tell them:

> Each small group will work together as a team to create loving messages, using the words from the list. The words may be used more than once. You don't need to use all the words. Designate one person to be the scribe for your group. Write as many phrases and sentences as possible.

Allow fifteen to twenty minutes for the groups to brainstorm and record their messages. Bring the groups together and invite them to read their messages out loud. Engage in conversation with these questions:

REFLECTION QUESTIONS:

- Does the group have a favorite message?
- What is your favorite as an individual?

Display the phrases and encourage participants to write additional statements throughout the retreat. You may wish to incorporate some messages into worship.

WORD LIST #1:

Beloved	This is	With	Pleased
Child	Whom	Commandment	Joy
You are	I	Give	Are
I am	Love	Encouragement	Harmony
God	Laugh	Each other	Connect
Light	New	World	Bless
Covenant	Shine	You	John 13:34
Genesis 9:9	Genesis 1:28	Matthew 5:14	

WORD LIST #2:

I	Mine	By name	You are
And	Called	Fear	I have
Been	God	Is	Love
One	Because	From	Another
Friends	Family	Strengthen	Restore
Fellowship	With	In	For
Yourself	Pray	Prayer	Isaiah 43:1

Group Gathering: Dream a Little Dream

Background:

In Genesis 37, Joseph's dreams inform him of his future prominence and power. When he shares this vision with his brothers, they are filled with jealousy and anger, which leads them to life-changing violence. How can we share our good news or dreams without diminishing those around us? How can we nurture our dreams when others do not share or support them?

Materials:

- Reflection questions
- Genesis 37:5–8
- Song: "Joseph's Dream"

Activity:

Participants have the opportunity to consider their own dreams and the impact those have on others.

Tell the group:

> Joseph had dreams that hinted at future greatness while outlining his family's diminished position; he would become a leader, and they would be in a position to need his power. The news that they would someday bow down to Joseph made his brothers furious.

Ask a volunteer to read Genesis 37:5–8.

Play the song "Joseph's Dream."

Provide participants with reflection questions; invite them to write their responses

REFLECTION QUESTIONS:

- What kind of dreams do you have for yourself? Where do you hope to be or what do you hope to do in the next three to five years?
- How will your dreams affect people in your life?
- Our dreams can change our situations, which can affect people in our lives.
- How do we nurture our dreams when others do not share them?
- Joseph's brothers felt threatened by his dreams. Is that the inevitable result of our visions, or is there another way to share our hopes of the future with others?

When participants have written their answers, divide into small groups (three to five people) to share responses. When the small groups have shared, bring the groups together to compare answers.

Group Gathering: Learning from the Past, Preparing for the Future

Background:

We know more about Joseph's childhood than almost any other biblical figure. We hear of the people and events that shaped his life and influenced his future; we even get to hear God speaking to him through his dreams. His story encourages us to reflect on our own journey as we consider where we have come from, where we find ourselves now, and wonder where God might be leading us in the future.

This activity offers an important opportunity for participants to apply the story's themes to their own lives.

Materials:

- Psalm 23
- Pens
- Song: "God Is My Shepherd" or other version of Psalm 23
- Worksheet for each participant

Activity:

Remind the group of Joseph's long life and how much he experienced and learned in his lifetime. Tell them they will have an opportunity to reflect on their lives as they consider what they have learned and where God may be leading them.

Tell the group:

> Psalm 23 reflects a life journey with ups and downs, peaceful moments as well as challenges. The promise of the psalm is that God will accompany us and provide for us along the way.

Play or sing "God Is My Shepherd."
Provide participants with the worksheet.

Worksheet (Divided into Three Columns So Participants May Reflect On the Growth and Movement Between Sections of Their Life Experience):

1. Childhood
   a. What nourished your joy?
   b. What made you feel proud or happy?
   c. What discouraged you or made you frightened?

2. Present
   a. Where are you growing?
   b. Where are you stuck?

3. Future
   a. What dream do you have for the future?
   b. What do you need from God for that to happen?
   c. What are good ways for you to share your dreams with others?

Allow time for them to answer the questions individually. Break into small groups for discussion.

Crafting Our Message: "I am . . ."

Purpose:

This craft encourages participants to define many facets of their identity by forming a sun which proclaims "I am" messages about their unique personality.

Materials:

- Posterboard for each person
- For each person: twenty to twenty-five strips of construction paper, each about twelve inches long
- Scissors
- Glue
- Magazines, greeting cards

Directions:

Instruct participants to draw a circle about five inches in diameter in the middle of their posterboard. In the center of the circle, instruct them to write the words, "I am."

Using words and images from the magazines, participants will glue descriptions of themselves onto the strips of construction paper. Encourage them to consider many characteristics of themselves. These might include roles (mother, nephew, daughter, sister, friend), character traits (strong, capable, funny, loyal), interests (a dancer, a gardener, a pursuer of beauty), hopes for the future (traveler, learner), and/or describing words (energetic, worrier, planner, part-time doubter). These statements can help reinforce the message that each one of us is a remarkable person created in God's image.

Several words, descriptions, or pictures can be placed on each paper strip. These should be glued around the center circle in the manner of rays of light, creating a sun effect.

Allow participants enough time to consider the depth and breadth of the many parts that comprise their personality. When participants have each created a sun, invite them to name some of their traits with others.

These can be placed in the worship area to celebrate all the unique personalities cherished by God.

Additional Craft Resources (for those who complete the craft early and are looking for further ideas):

- Adult coloring sheets (can be obtained free online)
- Colored pencils
- Pre-stamped postcards and pens (to be mailed by leader six to eight weeks after the retreat). Participants can write themselves a short note highlighting meaningful moments or quotes from the retreat.

Worship Resources:

These are themed resources to go with this particular retreat. Additional resources are available in the Appendix.

Litany (inspired by Psalm 23 and 130).

"A" and "B" can be divided by sides, birth months, ages, and so on.

A: Out of the depths I call to you.

B: From the pit of my despair and the pit of my stomach, I call out to you.

A: Out of the depths, in the midst of that dark valley, I search for you.

B: Let your ear be attentive to my voice. Please, hear me.

A; Remind me I am not alone.

B: I yearn for your comfort; I wait for your promise.

A: Even in the shadows, even when I am afraid.

B: I trust in your promise to always be with me.

A: Surely your goodness and mercy shall follow me, even pursue me.

B: All the days, every single day of my life.

Unison Prayer:

Joseph was tossed into a pit by people who were supposed to love him. I have been tossed and I have done the tossing. I know what it is like to be hurt by others. And I confess I know what it means to allow my heart to be hardened to the needs around me. When I am all too willing to turn my back, forgive me, Lord. Joseph's father favored him above all of his brothers. Some people are easier to love than others. Give me your compassion and help me to see with your loving eyes, so that I might love all my neighbors. Break into our imperfect world, Creator God, so that we may treat one another—and ourselves—with dignity and respect. Amen.

Chapter 7

Roots and Branches

Reflecting on Our Past, Preparing for Our future

About This Theme:

This rich retreat celebrates images of seeds, gardens, nature, and creation as participants explore their past (their "roots") and look toward the future (their "branches" or "growing edges"), all while giving thanks for those who have offered help and support along the way (the "gardeners of their lives"). Upon reflection, participants may be surprised to discover how God accompanied them through times of spiritual and emotional drought. Through conversation, prayer, journaling, and hands-on activities, they can explore God's promise to be with them as they grow into the unknown future.

This retreat allows participants to consider circumstances and people who shaped their roots. While some past growth provides sustenance for today, the rest needs to be trimmed or pruned to ensure a healthier plant. We may choose to build on strengths from yesterday or gain wisdom from choices we are determined not to repeat.

Reflecting on "branches" encourages participants to reflect on areas of growth and opportunity. Even when the branches are dormant, participants can visualize the hope provided by the God of new life.

This retreat is a celebration of life and God's faithfulness in every stage of our growth.

Scripture Focus:

- Psalm 1
- Jeremiah 17:7–8
- Matthew 13:1–9, 18–23
- John 15:1–5

"Quotable":

- "They are like trees planted by streams of water, which yield their fruit in its season, and their leaves do not wither" (Psalm 1:3).
- "I am like a green olive tree in the house of God. I trust in the steadfast love of God forever and ever" (Psalm 52:8).
- "I am the vine; you are the branches. If you remain in me and I in you, you will bear much fruit" (John 15:5).
- "The creation of a thousand forests is in one acorn."—Ralph Waldo Emerson

Introductory Objects and Bring-Along Items:

Invite participants to bring an object that speaks to them about the theme of "Roots and Branches." This small object will be shown to the whole group, so encourage participants to consider what they might be willing to share. Encourage people to use their imaginations as they decide whether to bring an actual root or branch that somehow represents them, or to offer a more symbolic offering that introduces their family tree or childhood home that provided their roots or foundation. There are no wrong answers—the objects that get presented will simply add to the community conversation!

In addition, encourage participants to bring quotes, short poems, or Scripture verses related to this theme to share during worship and group gatherings. This can be an engaging way to both learn more about one another and expand the repertoire of readings and songs during the retreat.

Leader's Tip:

Talking about the past (the root of our life) is not easy for everyone. Participants should be encouraged to self-select what they want to share or even reflect on during the retreat. While our roots are always part of our life story, they need not define our present or predict our future. We can choose how to care for ourselves today as we tend to our spiritual and physical well-being. Watch for people who may be temporarily overcome by a memory and need some quiet time alone or a private conversation. Plan a way for the retreat to continue if you need to offer support.

Music Resources:

Music can be interspersed throughout the retreat at mealtimes, the beginning and conclusion of group gatherings, and during worship.

Hymns:

- "De Colores (Song Of Colors)" (tune: "De Colores"). This toe-tapping hymn celebrates God's creation with Spanish and English lyrics.
- "God Of The Sparrow, God Of The Whale" (tune: "Roeder"). This very singable hymn reflects profound awe at the gifts of the Creator.
- "In The Bulb There Is A Flower" (tune: "Promise"). A song of resurrection and new life reminds the listener of the sometimes-hidden promises of God's faithfulness.
- "Like A Tree Beside The Water" (tune: "Silver Creek"). Inspired by Jeremiah 17:7–8, this lovely hymn compares us to trees seeking out God's nurturing strength.

Songs:

- "All Good Gifts" by Stephan Schwartz. From Godspell, a celebration God's generous bounty.
- "I Am The Vine" by Wild Goose Collective. Hauntingly beautiful tune in the Celtic tradition.

- "I Will Be The Vine" by Liam Lawton. This lilting, gentle tune echoes Jesus' words, "I am the vine, you are the branches" (John 15:5).
  - "In My Life" by the Beatles. Reflecting on those who were part of the past and still affect the present and future.
  - "The Sower And The Seed: Take Care Of Me" by John Hayles. The seed sings a song of needing God's care to grow. Found on YouTube.
  - "The Sower's Song" by Andrew Peterson. God tends to us so we can grow and offer our gifts.
  - "This Pretty Planet" by Tom Chapin. A children's song with powerful themes of caring for the earth, environment, and one another.

Video and Graphic Resources:

Search online for images of plants and trees growing in unlikely places, including:

- A tree with extensive root system growing on top of boulders, on a rocky hillside, or any location where the tree's root system must stretch and search for sustenance.
- A plant or flower growing through a crack in the sidewalk
- Cactus blooming in the desert

Print some of these images and place on larger sheets of paper. Invite participants to interact with the images by providing a caption or comment or adding their own drawing.

Creating the Atmosphere—Preparing Your Retreat Space:

- Display the schedule for your retreat in several places so it is easily seen by participants.
- Display posters with quotes that you have made.
- As much as possible, fill your space with living things (or pictures of them). One option is to invite participants to bring plants or flowers from home to help build the "roots and branches" theme.

Worship Area Suggestions:

When creating a worship area, consider including these items:

- Plants or flowers
- Roots, rocks, branches with or without leaves
- Flower bulbs
- Moss, ferns, air plants, succulents
- Watering can
- Small fountain with running water

Activities and Discussion Questions for Group Gatherings:

These gatherings can be used in any order, depending on the needs of the group and time constraints.

Group Gathering: Creating Storyboards

Background:

Jesus' parable of the Sower and the Seeds (Matt 13:1–9) offers a rich description of the impact of environment and living conditions on growth and health.

Materials:

- Copies of Matthew 13:1–9 for each participant
- Songs: "The Sower And The Seed: Take Care Of Me," "The Sower's Song"
- Tissue paper in a variety of colors
- Four pieces of rectangular posterboard, at least two feet by three feet
- Glue

Activity:

Tell the group that they will explore the story of the Sower and the Seed through music and the spoken word.

Listen to the song "The Sower And The Seed: Take Care Of Me." Invite conversation about the song by asking if any words or phrases caught their attention.

Invite a volunteer to read Matthew 13:1–9 to the group. Review the story by asking participants to describe the types of soils and dangers the seeds experienced. The participants will illustrate the story by creating storyboards. Divide into four smaller groups to represent parts of the story:

- Group 1: Birds
- Group 2: Rocky ground
- Group 3: Thorns
- Group 4: Good soil

Provide each group with the text. Tell the groups:

> Each group will create a picture of your part of the story by gluing torn pieces of colored tissue to form an image of the action. Think about what colors, shapes, and sizes are needed to depict the scene and convey the action. This is not meant to be a realistic picture, but rather a symbol of the story's message.

When each group has completed their storyboard, invite volunteers to put them in order. Ask a volunteer to retell the story (the group can help and encourage by adding words and phrases), using the storyboards as prompts.

The gathering can be concluded with "The Sower's Song," "In The Bulb Is A Flower" or another song.

Group Gathering: Getting "the Dirt" on the Sower and the Seeds

Background:

Jesus parable of the Sower and the Seed (Matt 13:1–9) is explained by Jesus (Matt 13:18–23).

Materials:

- Copy of Matthew 13:1–9, 18–23 for each participant
- Song: "The Sower's Song"
- Copy of discussion questions for each person (these may be split into two parts for separate discussion sessions)

Activity:

Invite the group to listen to "The Sower's Song."

Invite two volunteers to read the story of the Sower and the Seed and Jesus' explanation of the parable by reading Matthew 13:1–9, 18–23 to the group. Provide participants with the discussion questions. Say to the group:

> Everyone is invited to think about these questions on your own and write down your responses. Think about the parable we just heard and consider how it relates to your own life.

After allowing time for individual written responses (allow at least twenty minutes), you may choose to play a song and take a short break. When participants reassemble, form small groups (two to four people each) for conversation and sharing. Let participants know how much time they have to talk; encourage one person to be the timekeeper for the group to ensure everyone has an opportunity to share.

Encourage each participant to talk about the question(s) that are most meaningful to them; they do not have to discuss every question.

1. The "packed soil" is just not the right place to grow seeds.

   - When have you found yourself in a place, situation or job that isn't right for you?

   - What is "packed soil" for you?

   - How did you "uproot" yourself to find a healthier place to grow?

2. Some seeds fell onto "rocky ground."

   - What are examples of "rocky places" that we might encounter in life?

   - Describe one or two "rough patches" that you have experienced in your life.

   - What is a struggle that you have overcome or are working to overcome?

   - The birds come and pluck up the seeds. What (or who) have been some of the "birds" in your life? Where have you heard discouraging voices or met with resistance along your path?

3. The seeds had to try to grow around the rocks in the ground

   - The rocks can represent challenges in our lives that might hinder or discourage us. What are some examples?

   - What obstacles do you have to work around?

   - What is standing in the way of your growth or development? How can you respond?

4. Some seeds fell onto "thorny ground." The thorns limit growth and choke back new life.

   - Who or what has threatened (or perhaps has been successful) in holding back or limiting your choices or your growth? Who or what has tried to take away your dreams?

   - What distracts you from achieving your goals?

   - What saps your energy? How do you respond?

   - What helps to combat the thorns? Who or what encourages your dreams and hopes?

5. The seeds grew well in the good soil.

- What helps you grow? What strengthens your resolve or boosts your confidence?

- What can you do to feed your spirit? Nurture your hopes?

- What kind of atmosphere is good for you? How can you be proactive about creating a healthy environment for yourself?

Group Gathering: Gratitude for Our Gardeners

Background:

Few gardens grow without help. Plants thrive when they receive care, nourishment, and protection from dangers. This activity enables participants to consider who have been their helpful "gardeners" along their life journey.

Materials:

- Song: "All Good Gifts"
- Flower-shaped cutouts (paper, foam board, or similar material)
- Markers
- Stationary or greeting cards
- Pens

Activity:

Tell the group:

> As we consider our growth, we take time to celebrate those who have nurtured us along the way. Every living thing needs care and nourishment. We will take some time to give thanks for those who have offered us support. This song offers praise and thanksgiving for God's many blessings.

Play the song "All Good Gifts." Invite participants to consider the lyrics about plowing the fields and scattering seeds. Engage participants in a conversation about the "gardeners" in their lives by considering:

REFLECTION QUESTIONS:

- Who has helped you grow as a person?
- Who has provided encouragement along the way?
- Who has protected you from "weeds," or obstacles in your path?

Provide participants with the flower-shaped forms and invite them to write the names of at least one "gardener"—a person who helped them grow—and add a short description of the impact that person had. They may put more than one name on a flower shape or use multiple flowers.

When they have completed their flowers, invite participants to share reflections about at least one person who helped them develop into the person they are today.

The flowers can be collected and displayed on a wall or in the worship area to create a garden of gratitude.

Say to the group:

> Now that we have named some of the people who have offered support, we can express our gratitude by writing a letter to one of those people. Regardless of whether that person is still living, it can be a powerful exercise to articulate a sense of thanksgiving. Think about who you would like to thank and take some time to write a short letter of appreciation.

Provide participants with stationary; allow enough time to write letters. Emphasize that they may choose whether to actually mail the letter or simply hold on to it as a treasured reminder.

Group Gathering: Celebrating our Roots and Growing Edges

Background:

While the parable of the Sower and the Seed (Matt 13:1–9) describes the soil where a plant takes root, John 15:1–5 focuses on the plant's growth. Jesus' followers are described as "branches" who draw sustenance from the "vine," who is Jesus.

Materials:

- Pictures of grape (or other) vines to illustrate the Gospel story
- Line drawing or photograph depicting tree with roots and branches for each participant
- Copy of John 15:1–5
- Songs: "I Am The Vine," "I Will Be The Vine"
- Discussion questions for each participant

Activity:

Tell the group:

> Jesus tells us that he is the vine and we are the branches. Jesus describes how we grow in our faith and in our lives. We are not expected to produce anything on our own; instead, we are invited to draw our strength from Jesus. Our strength comes from his love.

Ask a volunteer to read John 15:1–5 to the group. Invite them to notice themes of this passage as they listen to the song "I Am The Vine."

Provide participants with a line drawing or a photograph of a tree that clearly depicts both the roots and branches. Invite everyone to take about ten minutes in silence as they look at the tree and consider the questions below. Invite them to take notes on the sketch for themselves; they do not have to share what they are discovering, but it is an opportunity for them to reflect on their own experience. As they read the questions, they may wish to label some of the roots and branches as part of their response.

Encourage participants to go beyond the easy answers that may come immediately to mind and to take the time to really consider the questions in as much depth as possible.

DISCUSSION QUESTIONS:

Consider your roots:

- Where did you grow up?
- Who lived with you?
- What fed your spirit as a child?
- What (and who) provided you with strength and encouragement?
- What roots and past experiences/relationships are you thankful for and wish to nurture?
- Although we cannot change the past, there may be parts of our past that we would like to cut off or "prune." Think about what those might be.
- If we cut off old roots, new ones may develop. Think about what new relationships or avenues feed your spirit and help you grow.

   Consider your branches:

- What's next in your life?

What are areas in your life that you would like to encourage to grow or expand?

- What will help you grow in the way that you dream about?
- Are there "branches" or habits/lifestyle choices that may no longer be healthy? Gardeners report that plants grow better when they are regularly trimmed, with unhealthy branches being pruned so that new growth may be established.
- What would you like to cut out of your life?
- What areas would you like to trim back?

Allow enough time (twenty to thirty minutes) to thoughtfully answer the questions. When participants have finished, you may wish to offer a short break.

When the group reassembles, play the song "I Will Be The Vine."

Divide into small groups of three to five people. Participants have an opportunity to know one another on a deeper level as they discuss the reflection questions. Invite them to share as they feel comfortable. This is not a time to relate one's entire life story so one person may need to act as a "spiritual timekeeper," in order to ensure time for each person to talk. Depending on the size of the groups, allow at least an hour for this time of discussion. Encourage participants to take the opportunity to listen and learn from one another. Each person can choose which and how many questions to discuss with the group.

When participants have completed their conversations, you may choose to have the group sing a hymn together before taking a short break.

Group Gathering: Trusting Our Roots, Celebrating Our Fruit:

Background:

The prophet Jeremiah recognizes periods of "drought" in our lives that can challenge our growth. By "rooting" ourselves in God, we can be nourished by God's love and support.

Materials:

- Newsprint and marker
- Copy of Jeremiah 17:7–8
- Butcher-block paper, at least five feet long (could also be several pieces of newsprint taped together)
- Markers
- Construction paper in many colors, cut in circles five inches wide. These will be the fruit.
- Construction paper cut in leaf shapes.

- Three-inch strips of paper, each twelve inches long. These will become the roots of the tree.
- Tape
- Songs: "Like A Tree Planted By The Water" and "De Colores"

Activity:

Create a "word cloud" on newsprint as a way to review what has been learned and discussed. Invite the group to call out words or short phrases ("growth takes time," "we need to be fed to grow," "thankful for caregivers") that reflect what they learned or discovered. Ask a volunteer to record all the responses. When everyone has had a chance to share, take a moment to look at the variety of responses.

The group can celebrate the strength God gives us by marveling at the power of the roots, which provide sustenance for the branches.

Tell the group they will create a visual representation of a tree. Tape the butcher-block paper vertically to the wall. Invite someone to draw the trunk of a tree by simply drawing two parallel lines down the paper.

Invite a volunteer to read Jeremiah 17:7–8 to the group. Tell the group that each person is one of those trees planted by the water. Each one of us is loved and nurtured by God. The passage suggests that drought and hardship will be part of life, but we can draw on God's strength and still flourish.

Listen to (or sing) "Like A Tree Planted By The Water." Invite the group to respond to the hymn and the Jeremiah passage by asking these questions:

REFLECTION QUESTIONS:

- Jeremiah says that anyone who has confidence in God will be like a tree planted by water. What is that kind of tree like? What gives someone confidence in God?
- The roots of the tree go into the stream so it will be protected from drought. Heat, danger, and hardship seem to be an inevitable part of life. If we can't avoid that, what can we do to protect ourselves?
- That tree by the water always produces fruit. What does that look like in a person? What are the signs of a spiritually healthy person?

Tell the group:

> We are going to take the time to construct a healthy tree. We already have the trunk. Now we are invited to shape the rest of the tree. There are materials to add roots, leaves, and fruits. These can be labeled with parts you think the tree needs—a root might be "time for myself" or "prayer," while a leaf might be "new opportunity" and a fruit might be "love," "power," or "possibility." Use your imagination—it's your tree!
>
> Think about what we have learned about the roots—what do we need in order to be well-rooted? Consider what kind of "fruit" will result when we are healthy and growing?

Invite participants to add as much to the tree as they would like. The intent is not to create a realistic depiction of a tree, but to celebrate Jeremiah's vision of a healthy creation nourished by God's love.

When participants have completed the tree, take time to read the written responses out loud and to marvel at this new creation. Invite any further comments or conversation.

Celebrate by playing or singing "De Colores," which praises the beauty of God's creation.

Crafting Our Message: Rooted in Love

Purpose:

Create a simple terrarium to offer participants the chance to literally sink their hands into the concept of roots and branches. As they tend to their plant at home, they can be reminded of God's continual care for each one of us.

Materials:

- Simple vase with a narrow top to limit moisture escaping. These can be found at a dollar store.
- Small rocks for the bottom of the vase.
- Planting soil.

- Small plants (can be obtained from a gardening center or florist; succulents are available inexpensively in bulk on Etsy).

  - Moss to help terrarium retain moisture.

  - Optional: small decorative rocks, figurines, ribbons.

Directions:

Tell the group:

> By creating a terrarium we will remind ourselves that we are all rooted in God's love. God feeds our spirits with healing, hope, and strength.

Invite a volunteer to read John 15:1–9 out loud. The terrarium can provide a living reminder of God's love for us.

Encourage the participants to take time to look at the supplies and consider what they would like to use in order to create a reminder of this retreat experience. Instruct participants to create their terrarium by placing small rocks in the base of the vase. Place some planting soil before gently placing the plant in the vase. Cover the roots and water. Participants may choose to add small decorative items to the terrarium or tie a bow around the top.

The terrariums may be added to the worship area as a living reminder of the retreat theme.

Additional Craft Resources (for those who complete the craft early and are looking for further ideas):

- Adult coloring sheets (can be obtained free online)

- Colored pencils

- Pre-stamped postcards and pens (to be mailed by leader six to eight weeks after the retreat). Participants can write themselves a short note highlighting meaningful moments or quotes from the retreat.

Worship Resources:

These are themed resources to go with this particular retreat. Additional resources are available in the Appendix.

Centering Prayer

Creator God, you have formed us in your image and have called us your beloved children. We gather in your name to nurture the Spirit you have placed within us.

- We thank you for the people and situations that we have left behind and offer them to your care. Please surround them with your love (silence for individual prayer).

- We give thanks for this time and this place. We ask you to slow us down so that we may receive the gifts that are offered here.

- Mindful of the beauty of your creation, we thank you for the many ways that you have nurtured our growth and encircled us with your love (silence for individual prayer).

Bless our time together as we gather for retreat. Remind us of our roots and help us to dream about our branches and pathways into the future.

Safe in your care, welcomed in your presence, we praise your holy name. Amen.

Call to Worship (Ps 8, NIV)

One: Lord, our Lord, how majestic is your name in all the earth!

All: You have set your glory in the heavens. Through the praise of children and infants you have established a stronghold against your enemies, to silence the foe and the avenger.

One: When I consider your heavens, the work of your fingers, the moon and the stars, which you have set in place, what is humankind that you are mindful of them, human beings that you care for them?

All: You have made them a little lower than the angels and crowned them with glory and honor.

One: You made them rulers over the works of your hands; you put everything under their feet: all flocks and herds, and the animals of the wild, the birds in the sky, and the fish in the sea, all that swim the paths of the seas.

All: Lord, our Lord, how majestic is your name in all the earth!

Litany (inspired by Jeremiah 17:7–8)

One: Blessed are those who trust in God.

All: We draw our strength from our Creator, like a tree planted by the water.

One: We send our roots by the stream, drawing nourishment from God, who loves us.

All: We shall not fear—even in hard times.

One: When challenges come, we will stand tall.

All: We draw our strength from our Creator, like a tree planted by the water.

Unison prayer (inspired by John 15:1–9)

Here we are, nurturing God, gathered in your presence, confident of your love and knowing that we are welcomed by you. You assure us that you are the vine and we are the branches; we can draw our strength from you. Sometimes our connection to you does not feel very strong. The storms of our lives can leave us feeling battered by circumstances and events. Our spirits are often parched as our energy wanes.

Renew us, Creator God. Feed our hungry spirits. During our time together, slow us down so that we may again hear your voice and be nourished by your Spirit. Open our hearts and our minds to you so that we may draw strength, encouragement, and wisdom from you. Let us sink our roots into the wells of your love and immerse ourselves in your transforming compassion. Rejuvenated by your love, help us bear good fruit and serve your world. Amen.

Chapter 8

Teach Us to Pray

Discovering Creative Spirituality

About This Theme:

How do you pray? When do you pray and how did you learn? And what is prayer, anyway? Defining prayer as a broad range of communication with God is a place to begin. Prayer can be spoken or silent; prayer can be us talking to God or listening for God's voice, which may be heard in a variety of ways.

As believers, we may have a desire to pray or think we "should" pray, but we often don't know where to begin. We assure people in need, "I will pray for you," but are uncertain how to do that or what affect it will have. We might recite memorized prayers, but they can often feel routine or empty. Sometimes we try to pray and get distracted or bored or simply feel less than satisfied. Sometimes we can't find time to pray and can feel slightly guilty at this perceived lack.

What if we were like the disciples and could make this request, "Lord, teach us to pray"? This retreat offers a time of discovery as participants experience a wide variety of prayer forms. They will have the opportunity to experiment with speaking to and listening for God through music, art, movement, silence, walking, journaling, and more. The retreat encourages participants to broaden their definition of prayer as they experience new forms of communication with God.

Scripture Focus:

Examples of Jesus praying:

- Luke 5:12–16
- Mark 1:35–39
- Matthew 6:5–13

Other examples of prayer:

- 1 Kings 19:11–12
- James 5:13–18

"Quotable":

- "[Jesus] was praying in a certain place, and after he had finished, one of his disciples said to him, 'Lord, teach us to pray, as John taught his disciples'" (Luke 11:1).
- "[Jesus] would withdraw to a quiet place to pray" (Luke 5:16).
- "Speak, Lord, for your servant is listening" (1 Sam 3:9).
- "You should sit in meditation for twenty minutes a day, unless you are too busy. Then you should sit for an hour."—Zen proverb
- "I have so much to do that I shall spend the first three hours in prayer."—Martin Luther

Introductory Objects and Bring-Along Items:

Invite participants to bring something that reminds them of God or the presence of God. Encourage them to consider if there is something they see in their daily life which reminds them of God or God's love and presence.

Tell participants that the retreat will offer opportunities for sharing so that we can learn about prayer from one another. The following items are not mandatory, but if participants would like to share, invite them to bring any of the following:

- A copy of a favorite prayer (if they have one) that they would like to share.

- A recording of a song that is meaningful to them or helps them pray or feel closer to God.

  - An instrument to play a favorite song.

  - A symbol that they pray with or to.

These items can be shared during worship times or at the beginning or ending of group gatherings.

In addition, tell participants that if they keep a journal, they are encouraged to bring it to the retreat.

Leader's Tip:

Remember your own bring-along object! Do you have something that reminds you of God's presence or helps you remember that God is with you?

Also: Think about your own prayer rituals and the ways that you pray. Be ready to talk about those—you don't have to be an expert on prayer, but everyone likes to hear personal reflections on what is helpful as well as struggles along the way. Your willingness to share your experiences and struggles will be an opening to others to reflect on their own experiences.

Make a poster with some definitions of prayer (look in a dictionary, Wikipedia, Google, or any denominational book of worship). Leave room on the poster so more definitions can be added during the retreat.

The book *Praying with Our Hands: 21 Practices of Embodied Prayer from the World's Spiritual Traditions* by Jon M. Sweeny offers photographs and short descriptions of prayer practices from across the globe. It provides some interesting food for thought as you prepare to talk about prayer.

Music Resources:

Music can be interspersed throughout the retreat at mealtimes, the beginning and conclusion of group gatherings, and during worship.

The diversity of these songs emphasizes the many types of prayer expressions available. Some are lively, toe-tapping praise rhythms, while others are heartfelt pleas for God's mercy and guidance. As the group explores the theme of prayer, these songs can help participants explore a variety of prayer modes.

Hymns:

- "Not My Brother, Not My Sister: Standing In The Need Of Prayer" (tune: "Need of Prayer"). This lively hymn can be sung as a "call and response" song, with the group repeating the phrase, "Standing in the need of prayer." It's a welcome reminder that no matter who we are, we all need God's blessing and help—and we are welcome in God's presence!

- "Out Of The Depths, O God, We Call" (tune: "Fennville"). This hymn reflects a time of agony, loss, despair—and the reassurance that God will not abandon in those moments.

- "Precious Lord, Take My Hand" (tune: "Precious Lord"). Known as the favorite hymn of Martin Luther King Jr., this song reminds us we can rely on God's strength and wisdom, especially when we do not feel equipped to face the challenges in front of us.

- "What A Friend We Have In Jesus" (tune: "Erie"). The repeated line reminds us to "take it to God in prayer." When we absent ourselves from God, we may experience a lack of peace and "needless pain." God is always ready to hear our prayers.

Songs:

- *For The Living Of These Days* by Kate Campbell. This album is comprised of hymns and songs related to prayer. Of particular interest might be "The Prayer Of Thomas Merton," a prayer set to music.

- "Forgive Us" by John McCutcheon. A reflection on the Lord's Prayer, particularly the challenge of forgiving others as we hope to be forgiven.

- "Morning Has Broken" by Cat Stevens. Found in many hymnals, this singable tune offers thanks for the beauty of God's creation.

- "Who Will Pray For Junior" by Kate Campbell. A poignant song about the power and importance of intercessory prayer. It can help us name the people for whom we pray—both those we know personally and those we hear about in the news.

- Songs from the Taizé Community (such as "Jesus, Remember Me" or "O Lord Hear My Prayer") can be taught or listened to either as an invitation into quiet time or as an example of meditation.

Creating the Atmosphere—Preparing Your Retreat Space:

- Display the retreat schedule so it is easily seen by participants.
- Display posters with quotes that you have made.

Worship Area Suggestions:

When creating your altar, you might include these items:

- A plant or flower
- A candle or electric votive
- A small plaque or wall hanging with a prayer

Activities and Discussion Questions for Group Gatherings:

These gatherings can be used in any order, depending on the needs of the group and time constraints.

Group Gathering: What Is Prayer?

Background:

Simply asking participants to define prayer and discuss their experiences with prayer can be a fascinating introduction to the topic. A variety of emotions can accompany a discussion of prayer—feeling inadequate or unprepared are not unusual sensations. This gathering encourages participants to explore the definition of prayer and how to experience it.

Materials:

- Newsprint
- Markers

Activity:

Say to the group:

> The goal of our retreat is to experience many different types of prayer. There are a variety of prayer forms that have developed throughout history and in different cultures. We will explore at least some of them.

Begin by asking the group to come up with a definition for the word "prayer." Ask a volunteer to record responses; then ask the question,

> How would you define prayer? What is prayer for you?

Remind them that there are no right or wrong answers, and there may be more questions than answers. As the responses are recorded, tell the participants that the retreat will allow them to explore their questions and experience a variety of ways to pray.

When they have shared their ideas about prayer, engage the group in conversation with these questions:

REFLECTION QUESTIONS:

- Did someone teach you to pray?
- Was prayer part of your family life as a child?
- Did you memorize any prayers?
- Do you have a time set aside for prayer? Do you pray "on the run"?
- Are there places that inspire you to pray?
- Do you have any frustrations with prayer or praying?
- What questions do you have about prayer?

Group Gathering: Experimenting with Prayer Forms

Much of this retreat is experiential as participants are introduced to a variety of ways to pray. A key component to this retreat is a relaxed atmosphere that invites participants to experience prayer forms and then reflect on them. This can be a time of exploration, questions, learning, and experimentation as participants experience some of the many types of prayer available.

It may be wise to discuss the vulnerability people might be feeling as they experiment with different forms of prayer. As leader, you can talk about creating a safe space where everyone is welcome to ask questions and try new forms of prayer (or not) as they encourage one another in their exploration of what prayer can mean to them.

As you introduce them to the prayer experiences, many of which may be new to participants, encourage them to be open to expanding their definition of prayer. Prayer can be much more than words quietly whispered to God as we kneel with closed eyes.

Throughout the retreat, participants can consider which prayer forms appeal to them and which they might choose to incorporate in their daily lives. Not every prayer form will appeal to everyone. Encourage the participants to consider this a "prayer buffet." They will be invited to try everything, and then can choose which prayer forms are a good "fit" for them. Encourage them to be open to experimenting and trying new ways to pray. After each exercise, take the time to check in with the participants. Encourage them to describe what that prayer form was like for them. Participants can often learn a lot from others' experiences; even if one particular prayer form does not "work" for them, they can appreciate how that prayer can touch someone else.

Several prayer methods are listed below. After reading the descriptions, you can choose to use all or some of them, allowing for some breaks or free time between prayer experiences. Some prayer forms include periods of silence and stillness, while other invite some movement or times of reflection and writing. You may choose the order in which the prayer methods are introduced based on the needs of your group. If long periods of sitting or silence will be challenging, you can invite them to experience a form that includes movement or conversation. You can gauge the needs of your group and choose prayer forms that will offer a wide variety of experiences.

Centering Prayer

Materials:

- Optional: bell or chime

This simple but powerful prayer form can be a good introduction to quieting the mind and relieving anxiety which can be done anywhere.

Tell the group to sit comfortably, with empty hands and relaxed bodies. Say to the group:

> We will begin with a few deep breaths. Be aware of your breath as you breathe in and out. As you breathe, you are invited to use a phrase or words to help you focus on the experience of simply being.

If some of the participants have experienced centering prayer previously, they may already have words or phrases that they use as they breathe in and out. For those who are experiencing this for the first time, you can suggest some phrases such as:

- I breathe in what is God, I breathe out what is not
- Here (breathe in) now (breathe out)
- God here (breathe in), God now (breathe out)

Tell the participants the group will sit in silence and experience this prayer form together for five minutes.

Invite the group to close their eyes and relax. As they breathe in and out, invite them to think of the word or phrase of their choosing.

After five minutes, ring a bell or simply say the word, "Amen." Ask the participants how they feel and what the experience was like for them.

Tell participants about the importance of taking time to slow down and enjoy even a few moments of silence and breathing each day. While some people recommend twenty minutes of centering prayer twice daily, even the smallest amount—like the five minutes just experienced—can be beneficial. Those precious moments can slow our heart rate, help us relax, and remind us of God's presence.

Sometimes people find it difficult to quiet their minds for even five minutes. The following exercise is (literally) a hands-on practice that can be used as an alternative to the sitting practice just experienced.

Say to the group:

> Hold up one hand with your fingers spread out. Take the
> other hand and very slowly trace the outline of one finger as
> you breathe out. Continue up the other side of your finger as
> you breathe in. You can say one of the words or phrases you
> just tried—or experiment with a different word or phrase.
> Continue until you have traced the outline of all five fingers.

Some people find the tactile sensation of outlining their fingers while
breathing in and out can help them focus on the practice. This simple practice can be used in school or at work, in the grocery line, or even in stopped
traffic. It can serve as a welcome reminder that in that moment, we are not
alone; God is there with us.

Lectio Divina

Background:

This ancient method of praying (often attributed to Saint Benedict in the
sixth century) may be especially appealing to those who enjoy reading,
working with words, or are comfortable with silent reflection.

Materials:

- Colossians 4:2–6 for each participant. Ideally, this will be printed on
  a page with double or triple spacing between lines so there is room
  for notes. The instructions outlined below should be printed on the
  same page.
- Pen for each person

Activity:

Tell the group:

> *Lectio divina* is Latin for "divine reading." This spiritual
> practice allows participants to mull over how God might be
> speaking to them through Scripture.

Tell the group that everyone will be given a copy of the same short Scripture passage. Remind them that God can speak to us through Scripture. This practice offers participants time to read, ponder, and listen to Scripture.

Before you hand out the paper with the Scripture, explain the following these steps:

Instructions for Lectio Divina:

1. Read the Scripture to yourself slowly. Pause.

2. Read the Scripture again.

3. Circle any words or phrases that attract your attention—they may appeal to you or cause you confusion.

4. Read the Scripture again.

5. Write down any questions or insights you have. Does any word or phrase seem to speak to you or remind you about any situation or circumstance in your life?

6. Take some time to think about the passage again and jot down any additional thoughts you may have. Ask the passage what it is trying to say to you.

7. When you feel done, come back to the group.

Allow up to fifteen minutes for this exercise. Once everyone seems finished, invite them to sit in small groups. Encourage them to share what they experienced, what insights they may have had, and what this form of prayer was like for them.

Music: Learning from the Psalms

Background:

The psalms invite participants to experience prayer through spoken and sung expression.

Materials:

- Psalm 150

- Simple, teachable refrain or short song that is known by you and easy to teach your group. Copies of the song may be distributed, or you may choose to teach the song by listening to it.

Activity:

Ask a volunteer to read Psalm 150 out loud. Encourage listeners to be aware of how many expressions of music this psalm contains.

Tell the group:

> Music has been part of prayer ever since people have prayed. Music is a vital part of worship throughout the Bible. One of the most familiar and favorite books of the Bible—the Psalms—is a collection of ancient songs. Although the original melodies have been lost, the lyrics are recorded as the Psalms and continue to be part of worship throughout the world. Music can be used in prayer and as prayer in many ways. People can listen to music or create music with instruments or voice.

Choose a simple song or refrain that is already known to many in the group or is easily learned. Ideally, this will be a song that can be sung from memory so that participants don't need to hold music.

Take the time to review the song until participants feel comfortable enough to put the music or lyrics aside. Invite them to focus on both singing and listening to the song.

Tell the group that they will sing the song several times. You can decide on the number of times, depending on the length of the song, but a minimum of three repetitions is recommended. Encourage the group to listen to the words of the song and also the sound of the voices around them. Remind them that this is not about being expert singers, but rather it is following in the ancient tradition of worshipers joining their voices together before God.

Tell the group:

> Often we can focus longer on prayer by singing. We might become more aware of particular words or phrases when we sing them rather than say them.

When the group has sung the song several times, ask participants how they feel and what the experience was like for them.

Music: Learning from Hymns

Background:

This prayer form involves listening to a song and reflecting on its lyrics. Hymn are an expression of creativity and inspiration. Much can be learned by researching what moved the composer and lyricist to create a particular hymn. When we sing (or even read) a hymn, we are benefiting from the creator's experience.

Materials:

- A song from the music resource list (or another of your choosing).
- Paper and pen for each participant

Activity:

This form of prayer reminds us that prayer involves more than speaking. An important part of prayer is listening and being open to hearing God's voice in different ways.

Choose a song or hymn from the list (or another favorite). Invite participants to sit comfortably. Explain that they will listen to a song and then respond to it.

Say to the group:

> As you listen to the song, jot down words or phrases that catch your attention. When the song ends, write a sentence or two to describe how the song makes you feel or what memories it may stir up.

Play the song again. Invite the group to sit in silence for two or three minutes as they again reflect on the song's message for them.

Invite participants to share what message or inspiration they heard. Participants may have very different impressions of the same song. Encourage them to reflect on why that is and what that might mean. Remind them that all of us arrive at a moment with our cumulative life experiences; these will influence what we hear and how it is received.

When everyone has had an opportunity to share, ask them if they can imagine hearing God's voice through music.

Object Lesson

Background:

Prayer does not have to be complicated. By using objects from God's creation, participants can reflect on (and communicate with) the Creator.

Materials:

A variety of objects from nature. These can include flowers, berries, roots, rocks, shells, feathers, small branches, leaves, driftwood, or anything that is easy to pick up. There can be several variations of the same object.

Activity:

Invite participants to look over the objects and to choose one that "speaks" to them, appeals to them, or makes them curious. Encourage them to take enough time to find an object that piques their curiosity or holds some meaning to them.

Invite participants to sit comfortably and to hold their object in their hand.

Tell the group:

> One part of prayer is opening our senses and being aware of the many ways that God might speak to us. This is an opportunity to use as many of our senses are possible as we listen to what one tiny part of God's creation may have to say to us.

There are three steps in this prayer experience:

1. Invite participants to take five minutes in silence with their object. Encourage them to use as many of their senses as possible. They can look at their object from many angles, they can feel its weight and shape, they can listen to any sound it may make, and they can smell it. While they may not want to actually taste their object (for health reasons, it's probably wise to avoid this), invite them to wonder about what that sense might tell them. Reassure them that they have plenty of time to get to know their particular object.

2. Invite participants to look at their object and to silently ask the questions, "What do you have to tell me? What can I learn from you?" Something may immediately come to mind, or it may not. Tell them that this is not something to be forced, but rather to pose the questions with a wondering mind. Invite them to consider what memories their object might evoke. Tell the participants they have three minutes to wonder about their object.

3. Invite participants to talk about their experience. Ask them to describe their object and encourage them to talk about what they experienced by spending time with this object.

When everyone has had an opportunity to share, remind them that prayer can be a series of questions. It can be a time to ask, "What can I learn from this situation or person?" We might be led to wonder, "What can I notice about this circumstance or object that may be helpful to me?" This method of prayer and reflective questions can help us to slow down and notice our surroundings instead of simply rushing through our day.

Praying with Art

Background:

This prayer exercise appeals especially to those who learn visually and/or respond to color and texture.

Materials:

- Reflection questions (listed on the next page)

- Four to six posters of paintings (purchased or found on Google Images, or another similar search engine). Try to find pictures from different cultures and styles with a variety of people and/or motifs. The art may be obviously "religious" or contain landscapes or symbols. Feel free to choose any art pieces; some suggestions might include Van Gogh's *Sunflowers*, landscapes by Grandma Moses, Andrew Wyeth's *Christina's World*, Greek Orthodox icons, pictures of stained glass windows, pictures of landscapes or groups of people/faces/hands.

  - If an artist will be attending the retreat, that person may be willing to talk about the inspiration that led them to create his/her piece. The act of listening to and responding to creative inspiration may be compared to the act of listening for the voice and inspiration of the Creator.

Activity:

Hang the art posters up around the room, leaving as much space between them as possible. Tell the group they will take the time to move about the room to look at each poster individually. After a few minutes, encourage them to pick one to study more closely.

Encourage participants to take time and observe as much about this piece of art as possible. Ask them to notice the colors, the shapes, the placement of people (if any), and any details that jump out at them.

Instruct participants to write brief answers to the following questions:

REFLECTION QUESTIONS:

- What made you choose this piece of art?
- What do you like about it?
- What don't you understand about it?
- If you could ask this art a question, what would it be?
- What story is this art telling you?
- Who or what are you in this picture?

After five to seven minutes, invite participants to come back and form small (four to six people) groups. Tell the groups to discuss the experience and to describe their encounter with a piece of art.

When everyone has had the opportunity to share, invite the group back together. Tell them that prayer can include listening and looking for God in unusual or unexpected places. Ask if anyone can briefly describe what "their" art work said to them.

Walking in God's Creation

Background:

God's creation—whether experienced outdoors or looking through a window—can speak to our spirits and inspire new understandings of our Creator.

Materials:

- Psalm 19:1
- Optional: bell or whistle

Activity:

Read Psalm 19:1 out loud.
   Tell the group:

> God's creation is repeatedly celebrated throughout Scripture. This prayer experience invites us to learn about the Creator by spending time in the creation.

There are many types of walking meditations and outdoor prayer forms. This particular one does not require extensive walking; rather, participants will be encouraged to go outside and find a comfortable place to sit or stand. This prayer form should be accessible to everyone and not exclude anyone with mobility concerns. The participants should not need to worry about managing their time, so tell them that you will ring a bell or blow a whistle when they need to return (you may also choose to designate a reassembling time). Encourage them to simply enjoy the experience of being outside without any responsibilities or any need to "produce" something.

Tell the group they will have the opportunity to go out into God's creation and will use their senses to be aware of God's presence.

Say to the group:

> In our daily lives, we often rush through creation or view it as something that must be tamed, manicured, or even feared. When we are driving, we may not notice the beauty that is all around us. If people have lawns or gardens, they may get caught up in the necessity of endless chores while not appreciating the unique beauty.
>
> This is an opportunity to simply be in nature.

Tell the participants that they will go outside in silence. They can look around for a place that appeals to them. Encourage them to stand or sit in that place and to use their senses to become aware of it, and to consider these questions:

REFLECTION QUESTIONS:

- What do I see?
- What do I smell?
- What do I hear?
- What do I feel?

Tell the participants that they will have ten minutes of quiet alone time. During that time, encourage them to wonder what this particular place might have to tell them. Since they have several minutes in one place, encourage them to really notice what is around them.

When ten minutes have gone by, ring a bell or blow a whistle to gather the group back together. Invite the group to reflect on the experience together.

Journaling

Background:

Writing can be a powerful form of prayer. Writing can slow our thoughts and offer perspective as we reflect on people and situations we wish to bring before God.

Materials:

- Two copies of Matthew 14:13–21 (feeding the Five Thousand)
- Pen for each person.
- Paper (or personal journal) for each participant.
- Reflection Questions for each participant

Activity:

Tell the group:

> The act of physically writing something can often engage our minds and spirits in a unique way. It can offer an alternative way to pray. Those who find their minds wandering when they try to pray silently may welcome the opportunity to jot down their thoughts, concerns, joys, and reflections. Writing can help us focus on a topic and actually bring about new discoveries.

Reassure the group that no one will read what they will write. They will not be graded or judged on their writing skill. This technique allows them to record their thoughts and feelings without trying to create a finished product.

Tell the group:

> As we listen to this Bible story, try to imagine the scene being described. Use your imagination to envision Jesus on the hillside preparing to feed thousands of people. Following the story, you will be offered some writing prompts to help you describe the experience in the story.

Invite a volunteer to read the story.

REFLECTION QUESTIONS:

Read the following questions without leaving time for comments:

- What was it like to sit on the hillside and listen to Jesus?
- How were the disciples feeling when they realized how little food they had?
- Do you ever feel like you don't have enough to offer?
- What would you like to ask Jesus to provide?
- There was lots of food left over. Is there any abundance in your life?

After a short pause, invite a second volunteer to read the same story again.

Provide participants with the reflection questions. Participants are not required to answer each question; instead, the questions should spark their own responses to the story.

Encourage the participants to write down their thoughts and not to worry if they seem to stray far from the original story or questions. They can journal anything that comes to their minds. It can be a list or a description. It can be addressed to God or themselves or someone else.

Tell them that they have ten minutes to enjoy a free-writing exercise.

When they have completed the exercise, engage in conversation about what the experience was like for them.

Crafting Our Message: Tools for Praying

Purpose:

There are two options for a craft that will create a tool to assist participants in their prayer life. Read over the descriptions of the crafts to see which one best suits your group.

Option 1: Prayer Calendar

Materials:

- Copy of prayer calendar for each participant (see "Worship Resources")

- Blank twelve-month calendar for each participant (can be downloaded free from Google Images or from other search engine)

Directions:

Tell the group that one way to incorporate prayer into our daily lives is to have a visual reminder to pray. A prayer calendar can help with this. Each participant can personalize the calendar with dates that are meaningful or significant to them. The calendar can be checked daily and prayers offered for the specific date or person listed on that date.

Option 2: Prayer Bracelet or Fob

Materials:

- Variety of beads—different shapes, sizes, colors
- Lightweight wire or thick craft string
- Sharp scissors or pliers to cut wire/string
- 3 x 5 inch index card for each participant

Directions:

Tell the group that many faith traditions use beads as a way to pray and to provide focus for meditation. In the Catholic tradition, people use rosary beads; in the Muslim tradition, ninety-nine beads represent the names for Allah, while in Buddhism, beads are used to help focus breathing practices and as an aid for repeating a mantra.

In a similar way, we can choose to use beads to remind us of particular people or situations that we would like to lift up in prayer. For example, someone may choose to have individual beads representing people for whom they pray. They may choose beads with a different shape or color to remind them of places, situations, or circumstances that need prayer. The beads can be strung on a wire in a circle to be worn as a bracelet or in a straight line to create a fob or bookmark.

Encourage participants to think about who or what they wish to pray. Invite them to create a key for the meaning of each of their beads (for example, the pink bead is for Aunt Rosie, the yellow bead for countries in poverty, and so on).

When participants have created their prayer bead craft, invite them to share the significance of their beads.

The prayer beads may be added to the worship center to remind participants about the power of prayer.

Worship Resources:

These are themed resources to go with this particular retreat. Additional resources are available in the Appendix.

Litanies

> Leader: Welcoming God, you invite us to come to you with all that is on our hearts and minds.
>
> People: You encourage us to pray every day, in every way we know how, for everyone we know.
>
> Leader: You welcome our pleas for help and strength, as well as our words of praise and thanksgiving.
>
> People: We offer you our prayers and intercessions, grateful that you care about the concerns on our hearts.

> Leader: Inviting God, you welcome us into your presence. How should we listen for your voice?
>
> People: Should we be like Samuel and say, "Speak Lord, for your servant listens."
>
> Leader: Will we be like Saul and be knocked to the ground by the power of your voice?
>
> People: Or will we be like Elijah and hear you speak to us in a still, small voice?
>
> Leader: Open our hearts and our spirits to you, the living God.
>
> People: God who speaks in stillness, help us to hear your voice and receive your guidance.

Unison Prayers

Here we are, Lord, standing in the need of prayer. We pray for our brother and sisters and also for ourselves, that we may know your will and follow in your way. Thank you inviting us to lay our burdens down and entrust our cares to you. Forgive us when we think we have to shoulder every problem alone and struggle on through life without help. Remind us that you journey with us and guide us like a good shepherd. As you care and nurture us, help us to offer care and comfort to your children all around us. In Jesus' name we pray. Amen.

Living and loving God, sometimes we are like Saul and only think that we are doing the right thing. Sometimes our words and our actions are displeasing to you. Sometimes we might need to be knocked off of our high horse before we are willing to listen to you. Forgive us for being so busy that we cannot hear you and for being so sure of ourselves that we do not even ask you if we are pleasing you. Interrupt our multitasking lives and help us to simply listen. Fill us with your guidance and new life so that we can share the hope that you offer every day. Amen.

Loving God, you speak to us in so many ways. We can hear your voice in the wind whispering through the trees. We can sense your majesty in the stars blinking in the night sky. You are always inviting us to come closer, to see and know your glory, and to receive your good news. Yet there are times when we don't recognize your voice. We don't always hear your call. We often find ourselves filled with doubt or are simply not sure how to follow you. We thank you, loving God, that you have more confidence in us than we often do in you. Open our ears and our hearts that we may hear you. Free our tongues and our spirits that we may share your good news with everyone we meet. In Jesus' name we pray. Amen.

Prayer Calendar

Your prayers can be inspired by events, past, present, and future. Here are some "prayer starters" based on the calendar dates. Personalize your own calendar using events from this list and adding your own significant dates, anniversaries, and occasions

January

- New Year's Day: Prayers for unknown future, those hoping for changes in their lives or circumstances in the New Year.
- Martin Luther King Day: Prayers for those working for justice and peace and for those who live with inequality in their lives
-
-

February

- Presidents' Day (United States): Prayers for our leaders in local, state, and national offices. Prayers for world leaders working for peace and improved circumstances in their countries.
- Valentine's Day: Do you have someone who loves you? Give thanks for that person. Who are the people who are close to your heart? Ask for God's guidance, wisdom, and protection to be with them. Remember also those who are mourning the loss of a loved one and whose hearts may feel empty on this day.
-
-

March

- Saint Patrick's Day: Pray for peace in Ireland and all countries torn apart by religious or cultural differences
- First Day of Spring: Pray for farmers and all those who depend on the earth to make their living.
-
-

April

- Beginning of baseball season: Pray for professional athletes and also for all the children who will be participating in sports. Remember the parents and grandparents who will be providing transportation. Pray for balance in the lives of busy families.

-

-

May

- Mother's Day: Pray for mothers everywhere. Give thanks for your mother, or whoever helped raise you as a child. Pray for motherless children in this country and around the world. Pray for those who have difficult relationships with their mothers. Pray for those whose mothers have died. Pray for those who hoped to have children but were unable to do so, and the way this holiday may make them feel.

- Memorial Day: Pray for those in the military who are serving in this country and overseas. Ask God to give their families the strength and courage that they need.

- If you live in a country that enjoys freedom and liberty, give thanks for those blessings. Remember those who live under tyrannical regimes and people who wake up afraid every morning.

-

-

June

- Father's Day: Pray for wisdom, strength and patience for fathers everywhere. Give thanks for your father, or whoever raised you as a child. Pray for fatherless children across the globe. Pray for those who have difficult relationships with their fathers. Pray for those whose fathers have died. Pray for those who hoped to have children but were unable to do so, and the way this holiday may make them feel.

- End of school: Pray for students who are graduating and beginning a new chapter in their lives.

- Pray for families whose schedules will change as school ends; ask God to be with single mothers, grandparents raising children, families who need childcare, and those who can't afford to provide safe care for their children.

- As more young drivers will be on the road, ask God to guide them and keep them safe.

-

-

July

- Independence Day (United States): Pray for your country, its leaders, and its citizens. Pray for peace among nations, and greater understanding among cultures and religions.

-

-

August

- Pray for those experiencing different seasons in the world. As the northern hemisphere is enjoying summer, the southern hemisphere is in the midst of winter.

- Pray for those affected by the extremes of nature: heat, cold, hurricanes, earthquakes, tornadoes, flooding, and so on.

-

-

September

- Beginning of school: Prayers for teachers and all those who guide and influence young lives. Pray for children you know.

- Labor Day: Prayers for those whose hard work make daily life run smoothly. Pray for construction workers, day laborers, factory workers, and people whose labor is often unseen—miners, oil rig workers, deep sea fishermen, and astronauts. Who else can you name?

- Rosh Hashanah and Yom Kippur: Pray for our Jewish brothers and sisters. Ask God to help us live together in peace with people of all faiths.

-

-

October

- Columbus Day or Indigenous Peoples' Day: Pray for original peoples in all countries, those who are often overlooked, exploited, or forgotten, and whose traditions and ways may not be respected or understood.

- Thanksgiving (Canada): During this harvest time, pray for farmers and farm workers.

- Halloween: Pray for children everywhere. Give thanks for surprising "treats" in your life.

-

-

November

- All Saints' Day: Take a moment to remember a loved one who is no longer living. Consider what a difference that person made in your life, and give thanks for the difference that person made to you.

- Thanksgiving (United States): Make a list of ten things for which you give thanks. Think of someone who is struggling, and consider what you might do to help that person.

-

-

December

- World AIDS Day: Pray for all those affected by HIV/AIDS and for their caretakers.

- Pray for all those affected by chronic illness and for their families.

- Christmas: Ask God to allow God's peace, love, and hope to be reborn in your heart. Think about ways that you can share the good news of the God who dwells among us.

- Think about Mary and Joseph. Pray for those who are afraid or in danger.

- Jesus was born in rough conditions. Pray for those who are homeless and hungry.

- Offer prayers for the many religions celebrating holidays this month.

-

-

Chapter 9

Created in God's Image

Affirming Ourselves and Welcoming Others

About This Theme:

In a world that often encourages conformity and discourages unique expressions of self, this retreat celebrates each one of us as a beloved child of God. Instead of turning away from our differences, participants are encouraged to develop a "holy curiosity" about themselves and others.

It is too easy to dismiss our own gifts and value. When we compare ourselves to others, we falsely believe that we come up short. The pervasive drone of social media and advertising can convince us that we are lacking. These demoralizing falsehoods can eat away at our confidence and undermine self-esteem and self-worth.

Taking time to listen to one another's stories can help participants recognize existing differences and similarities while appreciating each person's distinctive natures. On this retreat, participants learn about their God-given identity and how their unique story adds to God's creation.

Both youth and adults can benefit from the chance to discover more about their unique value. Whether participants are long-time friends, a newly formed group, or a mixture of both, this retreat will offer opportunities for everyone to listen to and honor one another's stories.

Scripture Focus:

- Isaiah 43:1–2
- Matthew 10:40–42

"Quotable":

- "Do not fear, for I have redeemed you; I have called you by name, you are mine" (Isa 43:1).
- "Jesus said, 'Whoever welcomes you welcomes me'" (Matt 10:40).
- "You are my beloved" (Mark 1:11).
- "Never bend your head. Hold it high. Look the world straight in the eye."—Helen Keller
- "Outside show is a poor substitute for inner worth."—Aesop

Introductory Objects and Bring-Along Items:

Invite participants to bring an object that represents something about themselves—a hobby or pastime, a topic they are interested in, an experience they have had, or a dream that they cherish. Remind them that this does not have to be religious in nature—just something about them.

In addition, encourage participants to bring quotes, short poems, or Scripture verses related to this theme to share during worship and group gatherings.

Leader's Tip:

Remember your own object! Think about what you would like to share with the group that will provide some insight into who you are and what your interests are.

Music Resources:

Music can be interspersed throughout the retreat at mealtimes, the beginning and conclusion of group gatherings, and during worship.

Hymns:

- "Blessed Be The Tie That Binds" (tune: "Dennis"). An old (1782) hymn with a modern message. Bound together by God's love, we can share one another's burdens.

- "Help Us Accept Each Other" (tune: "Aurelia"). God's loving acceptance of us inspires us to welcome one another.

- "Song Of The Saints Of God" (tune: "Grand Isle"). This lively song celebrates diversity among God's people and rejoices that we are all "saints of God"!

- "Jesu, Jesu, Fill Us With Your Love" (tune: "Chereponi"). When filled with Christ's love, we can love and serve our neighbor.

- "O For A World" (tune: "Azmon"). Despite our differences, this simple hymn envisions a time and place where "everyone respects each other's ways."

Songs:

- "Christmas In The Trenches." Several versions of this haunting song tell the story of a temporary World War I truce that allowed enemies to put aside their weapons and celebrate Christ's birth. How can we overcome barriers that separate us?

- "Doors Of Heaven" by Arlo Guthrie. What would it be like if all of us were forced to live together and find a way to get along?

- "I Like The Things About Me" by Mavis Staples. A powerful song that encourages listeners to appreciate their unique abilities and qualities. Although she "used to despise" some aspects of herself, Mavis Staples now celebrates her individuality and self-worth.

- "If You Want To Sing Out" by Cat Stevens. This song celebrates every individual's right to express unique gifts and abilities.

- "Strangers Like Me" by Phil Collins, from the Disney movie *Tarzan*. Brought up in completely different circumstances, Tarzan and Jane recognize there is "much to learn" from and about one another. This upbeat song encourages curiosity about one another, as well as willingness to listen and learn.

- "What If We Are One" by Pamela Chappelle. This beautiful folk song asks us to ponder "what if our differences mean nothing at all" and provides a vision of all people as "one."

  - "You Are Mine" by David Haas. God's tender love expressed in Isaiah 43:1 forms the bases of this beautiful song.

Creating the Atmosphere—Preparing Your Retreat Space:

- Display the schedule for your retreat in several places so it can be easily seen by participants.

- Display posters with quotes that you have made.

- Hang up a mirror labeled, "You are a beloved child of God."

Worship Area Suggestions:

When creating your altar, you might include these items:

- Baby name book

- A list of participants' names on a sheet of paper entitled, "Beloved Children of God"

- Space for participants to place their bring-along objects

Activities and Discussion Questions for Group Gatherings:

These gatherings can be used in any order, depending on the needs of the group and time constraints.

Group Gathering: What Is Your Name?

Background:

What we are called—and how we name ourselves—is an important aspect of self-identity. This activity offers participants an enjoyable way to discover more about their own names while marveling at the loving identity—beloved child—God bestows on each one.

Materials:

- Matthew 3:16–17 in three translations
- Newsprint
- Markers
- Tape
- Paper for each participant
- Pens
- Baby name books: there should be enough for participants to easily share. These can be borrowed from the library or congregation members, or purchased used online very inexpensively.
- Reflection questions

Tell the group:

> We will be learning about the power and significance of our names. We are told that God knows each one of us by name. We are never strangers to God. We always have the identity God gave us—each of us is a beloved child of God. We will be listening to the story of Jesus' baptism when Jesus was named publicly by God. This story demonstrates how Jesus was identified by God. We will listen to three translations of the same verse. Listen for the differences and similarities between them. Try to notice the name or names that Jesus is given when he is baptized.

Invite three volunteers to read a translation of Matthew 3:16–17. Having different voices read the translations can help the group listen to the variations in the translations.

Ask the group what names they heard given to Jesus. Write the names on newsprint. Some examples might be "my Son," "my beloved," "the delight of my life," or "the one with whom I am well pleased." Take some time to talk about these names. Lead the group in conversation with these questions:

REFLECTION QUESTIONS:

- Which name do you prefer?

- Does any name surprise you?

- Is any name particularly significant to you?

Tell the group:

> Each one of us is given a name by God that can never be taken away; each one of us is named "beloved child" of God. No matter what anyone else might say about us or how they might describe us, this will always be true about us—we are known and loved by God. During the retreat, we will explore the idea of our God-give identity.

Form groups of six people or fewer to allow for enough time for each person to share.

Give each group two or three baby name books and invite people to look up information about their own names. Encourage them to compare the information found in different books.

Provide each group with discussion questions. Encourage them to use the questions to engage in a conversation where everyone has the opportunity to speak.

DISCUSSION QUESTIONS (ALLOW AT LEAST THIRTY MINUTES, DEPENDING ON GROUP SIZE):

1. What information did you find in the baby name books about your name?

2. Is there a story about how you were named? Were you named after someone; does your name have any family history or significance?

3. Do you like your name? Have you ever wished you could change your name?

4. Have you ever had a nickname? Nicknames can be endearing or hurtful. How did you get that nickname? Was it a positive or negative experience?

Almost everyone has a story or a strong feeling about their name. You may wish to take the time to bring the whole group together to share some of these stories and discuss the reflection questions before moving on to the next part of the activity.

Following the conversations, invite each person to write the name they wish to use during the retreat on the top of an 8.5 x 11 inch piece of paper (hold the paper vertically so there is more room left below the name). This may be the name that the person has been given, or may be a name of their choosing that they wish to try out during this shared time.

Invite participants to display these papers together so they are visible throughout the retreat.

Encourage participants to write on each other's papers throughout the retreat experience. Tell the group:

> You have the power to support one another with positive messages. In the same way that God always calls us "beloved child," we are invited to offer words of encouragement and hope. During the retreat, you are invited to write descriptive words or phrases ("kind," "always ready to listen," "lovely smile"), quotes, words of encouragement, or even add a drawing or sketch. Be sure to write on everyone's paper.

Note to leader: monitor this interaction to ensure that everyone is receiving positive messages and that no one is excluded. Remind participants about this activity throughout the retreat.

Group Gathering: Strangers Becoming Friends

Background:

It is a wonderful experience to be among people who know and appreciate you. Often, however, we find ourselves among strangers or in situations where we may not feel completely comfortable. Breaking down barriers and discovering ways to meet and appreciate one another can be a powerful experience.

Materials:

- Song: "Strangers Like Me" or another song of your choice
- Newsprint
- Markers
- Tape
- Reflection questions

Activity:

Ask the group to think of a time when they were in a group of strangers; situations like the first day of school, starting a new job, or moving to a new location might come to mind. Invite them to listen to the song "Strangers Like Me," which describes a curiosity and growing interest in getting to know a stranger.

Play the song and engage the group in conversation by asking:

REFLECTION QUESTIONS:

- What is it like to be a stranger?
- Have you ever been in a group of strangers who starting talking with one another? What made that possible?
- Sometimes we are in a group of strangers, and sometimes we might be the only stranger in the room. How are those situations different? Which would you prefer?
- Are you good at remembering people's names? How do you do that?
- What is it like when someone can't seem to remember your name? What does that feel like?

Group Gathering: A Timeline of Your Life

Background:

Participants will map out their life's journey as they reflect on God's presence and guidance.

Materials:

- Paper (at least 8.5 x 14 inches or longer) for each participant
- Markers, pens
- Tape
- Psalm 23 for each person, in several translations
- Reflection questions on newsprint or for each participant
- Song: "I Like The Things About Me"
- Lyrics: "I Like The Things About Me" for each participant

Activity:

Tell the group:

> Psalm 23 is the story of someone's experience through the good and bad, the ups and downs of life. Listen to the psalm and try to imagine both the positive and challenging moments that are being described.

Invite the group to read the psalm together. Then ask volunteers to read other translations to the group.

Tell the group:

> During the psalmist's life, there were ups and downs, twists and turns. How would that look if we tried to map this life out?

Demonstrate to the group how to make a life timeline: at the farthest lefthand side of the paper, make a mark to illustrate that person's birth. Let the participants know that there is much that we don't know about the psalmist's life, but we can use the clues given to us to describe some main events in his/her life.

Ask the participants to name some of these events. Participants might include "dark valley," "green pastures," or "a table set in front of enemies." Mark these on the timeline.

Say to the group:

> Everyone has a unique story with twists and turns. We will listen to a song that encourages us to appreciate our abilities and qualities. Exactly those times when everything was going wrong—our personalities were being formed. We have become the people we are today because of what we have experienced.

Play the song "I Like The Things About Me" as participants read the lyrics.

Provide participants with paper, pens, and markers. Invite everyone to create a timeline of their lives that includes significant events along the way. Reassure participants that this does not need to include any actual drawing. They can use markers and/or colored pencils to illustrate both the highlights and "lowlights" of their lives.

Encourage them to consider these questions as they create their timeline:

REFLECTION QUESTIONS:

- Where did you grow up? Who took care of you?
- Were you part of a faith community? What was that like?
- How often have you moved? Did you have a favorite place?
- What are some favorite memories?
- Where were some "green pastures" or "dark valleys" for you?
- Do you have dreams for the future?

Let them know that they will only need to share the parts that they feel comfortable discussing; the retreat offers a safe space where everyone is able to choose what they do or do not wish to share.

Once everyone has completed their timeline (this can take up to thirty minutes), divide into smaller groups (two to four people). Tell the groups to designate someone to act as a timekeeper so everyone will have the opportunity to talk. Encourage each person to share his/her timeline or a portion of it.

Leader tip: You can help the groups by giving gentle reminders about time management and encouraging everyone to speak.

Group Gathering: Evolving Identity—How Do We Grow and Change?

Background:

By considering their God-given name ("beloved child"), participants celebrate their identity.

Materials:

- Basin or bowl of water
- Hymn: "Help Us Accept Each Other," "Jesu, Jesu," or another hymn

Activity:

Invite the group to sit in a circle around the basin of water and sing (or listen to) one of the listed hymns or another of your choice. The basin should be easily accessible on a table at waist height.

Tell the group:

> We are all different from each other. We each have an identity, but the way that we think about ourselves can change as the years go by. There are times in our lives when our identity changes or shifts. Different chapters or events invite us to think of ourselves in new ways or to discover some new aspect about ourselves. Sometimes it is because of a dramatic event, and other times it is a gradual evolution of attitudes and outlooks. Sometimes life events alter the way we identify ourselves. For example, the birth of a sibling causes us to be named "brother" or "sister," the death of our parents lead to our identity as "orphan" or "parentless," or moving to a new community may cause us to be named as "stranger," "newcomer," or "outsider."

Our identities evolve as we learn and experience new things. If we discover a new hobby or talent, we may rename ourselves as "singer" or "artist" or "crafter." If we delight in learning something new, we may name ourselves "explorer" or "student."

Invite the group to listen to examples from the Bible when someone's identity was changed because of their life experience. In these stories, the name of the person often changes; indicating that they may be embarking in a new direction or engaging in a new task Ask volunteers to read Genesis 17:1–5, 15–16 and Genesis 32:22–28. Engage the group in conversation with these questions:

REFLECTION QUESTIONS:

- What name change did you hear?
- What will new thing is happening in that person's life?
- Have you ever experienced a time when your name or title changed to reflect a new or different identity? What was that like for you?

Ask participants to think of a word or phrase that might describe them as they are now. Give them one or two minutes to think about this. Then say:

> Now think of a word or phrase that describes a future identity. Maybe it will be an attitude that you wish to adopt, a change you wish to celebrate, or even a prayer for the future. Maybe you have a new way you would like to think about yourself. We can be inspired by the story of Jesus being named at baptism, as well as the stories of biblical people receiving a new name at an important juncture of their lives.

After giving time for reflection, tell the participants:

> We are going to celebrate that God is always doing something new in our lives. You can celebrate your new/growing/evolving identity by claiming that identity or name.

Explain to the group that they will move forward to the bowl of water, dip in their fingers, and touch their forehead. They are invited to say their name and state their new/growing/evolving identity. Encourage them to say it out loud, but participating silently is fine, as well. Because this is an individual experience, there are no right or wrong ways to do this. This is an opportunity for everyone to claim an identity and to celebrate their irrevocable status as a beloved child of God.

Some possible examples include:

- I am Sue, beloved child of God, who yearns to be a traveler.
- I am Patti, beloved child of God, a knitter and creator.
- I am Roger, beloved child of God, healthy and at rest.

Individuals may go forward in any order, and people can participate at will (or even participate silently in their place).

When you have the sense that everyone who wishes to participate has done so, you may close this time by saying:

> May the God of yesterday and today, the God who is already in tomorrow, bless us on our journey and surround us with peace. Amen.

Crafting Our Message: Candle Mosaics

Purpose:

Create a decorated candle that symbolizes our unique identity and celebrates God's light shining through us.

Leader's Tip:

It's a good idea to have a sample to show participants so they can anticipate what the finished product should look like.

Showing participants a book by Eric Carle such as "The Hungry Caterpillar" can offer a good example of this style of design.

Materials:

There are two options for this craft.

1. Create a mosaic jar which will hold a votive candle
2. Decorate a pillar candle with a mosaic pattern

Option 1: Decorated mosaic jar:

- Clean, clear glass jar for each participant
- Tissue paper, in as many colors as possible.
- Modge-podge glue
- Small cups to hold individual amounts of glue
- Small inexpensive, disposable paintbrush for each participant
- Paper towels

Option 2: Decorated pillar candle:

- Short (three to five inch) pillar candle for each participant
- Tissue paper, in as many colors as possible.
- Modge-podge glue
- Small cups to hold individual amounts of glue
- Small inexpensive, disposable paintbrush for each participant

Activity:

Read Matthew 5:14–16 out loud.
   Say to the group:

> Jesus tells us that we are the light of the world and that this light should not be hidden, but rather shared for all to see. Christ's light shines in a unique way through each one of us. We are given God's love and light and invited to share those gifts with others. As we create our mosaic crafts, we can express our individuality.
>
> When we are finished, we will be amazed at how different each craft looks, even though we are all using the same materials. Those differences should make us curious about one another as we continue to listen and learn.

Directions:

Each participant should take a candle or jar, tissue paper squares, a small cup of glue, and a paintbrush.

Invite everyone to decorate their jar or candle using any colors or patterns they choose. Apply glue liberally to the surface. Place tissue paper in single layers to the glue. Thin layers will be more aesthetically pleasing and will allow light to shine more easily through the colored paper. Participants may choose to create a scene by cutting out shapes (sun shining on water, for example) or create a stained-glass effect by using small pieces of tissue together.

Additional layers can be added to create a colorful mosaic. Glue is applied between each layer, as well as on the entire surface. The glue will dry clear.

Explain that this craft represents their individual personalities, so there is no right or wrong way to do this.

When participants have completed their craft, invite them to share the significance of their mosaic.

The completed crafts can be added to the worship area to celebrate God's light shining through each participant.

Worship Resources:

These are themed resources to go with this particular retreat. Additional resources are available in the Appendix.

Call to Worship (Inspired by Hymn "Jesu, Jesu" and Matt 10:40–42):

> One: Caring God, fill us with your love. Show us how to serve the neighbors.
>
> Many: Let us be inspired by Jesus, who knelt at the feet of those in need.
>
> One: Open our eyes to recognize our neighbors as beloved children of yours.
>
> Many: Open our hearts that we share your compassion with others.
>
> One: Let us worship and serve you with our actions and our deeds.
>
> Many: Let us serve you in the Spirit of our Servant Savior, Jesus.

Celebration of Our Diverse Gifts (Inspired by 1 Cor 12):

> One: For the mosaics of our lives, patterns of people, and experiences that enrich us, we give you thanks.

> Many: For bringing all these different people, opinions, and backgrounds together to form your church, we thank you.

> One: For calling us the body of Christ, consisting of endless varieties of gifts and talents, we give you thanks.

> Many: Creator and creative God, open us to your spirit and bring us together to form a vision of your new life and hope.

Unison Prayer:

God of compassion, you welcome us every day. When we are more willing to receive than to give your kindness, have mercy on us. Help us to be inspired by Jesus, who was able to look beyond disease, status, and social barriers in order to share transformation, hope, and new life. Fill us with your Spirit of generous hospitality, that we may live your gospel of welcome and love. Amen.

Chapter 10

Wherever You Go

Celebrating Special Relationships

About This Theme:

This retreat focuses on relationships of particular significance. Participants are invited to attend with one or more people who are meaningful to them. Relationships of all types—parent/child, friends, partners, spouses, siblings, neighbors, teammates—enrich our lives. This retreat celebrates the significance of those bonds and invites participants to appreciate their life-giving nature. Our busy schedules don't offer opportunities to pause and appreciate the people who make a profound difference in our lives

Participants will have the opportunity to look back at their relationship's history and recognize its ongoing significance. This retreat provides participants with the opportunity to joyfully express their appreciation for one another as they ponder how this relationship impacts and enhances their lives. Our human connections are a reflection of God's love and caring; this is a chance to express gratitude for this relationship.

Although some time will be spent with the entire group, much of the retreat concentrates on the specific relationships of those attending the retreat together. Participants register in groups of two or more, and should plan to attend together. Because of the variety of relationships, these are referred to as relationship groups.

Note to leader: the unique nature of this retreat requires some forethought and planning. It may be helpful to offer help with childcare, or offer a reduced rate for families to encourage participation. Thoughtful consideration should be given to the wide variety of relationships and family groupings that exist today. The leader should take care to advertise and provide a safe space which allows everyone to attend.

Scripture Focus:

- Genesis 2:15–24
- Exodus 4:10–17, 15:20
- Ruth 1:16–17
- 1 Samuel 18:1–4
- Matthew 4:18–22

"Quotable":

- "Then the Lord God said, it is not good that the man should be alone; I will make him a helper as his partner" (Gen 2:15).
- "Where you go, I will go; where you lodge, I will lodge; your people shall be my people, and your God my God" (Ruth 1:16).
- "The Soul of Jonathan was bound to the soul of David" (1 Sam 18:1).
- "I am my beloved's and my beloved is mine" (Song 6:3).
- "Love is patient; love is kind; love is not envious or boastful or arrogant or rude. It does not insist on its own way; it is not irritable or resentful; it does not rejoice in wrongdoing, but rejoices in the truth. It bears all things, believes all things, hopes all things, endures all things" (1 Cor 13:4–7).
- "We love because God first loved us" (1 John 4:19)
- "How very good and pleasant it is when kindred live together in unity" (Ps 133:1).
- "If I have seen further than others, it is by standing upon the shoulders of giants."—Isaac Newton
- "Alone we can do so little. Together we can do so much."—Helen Keller

Introductory Objects and Bring-Along Items:

Invite participants to bring pictures of their relationship or mementos of experiences shared. They might also like to bring an object that represents their relationship.

In addition, encourage participants to bring quotes, short poems, or Scripture verses related to this theme to share during worship and group gatherings.

Leader's Tips:

Be sure to bring your own representative object or picture so you can share about one of your special relationships.

Prior to the retreat, inform participants that they will be discussing their family tree or the history of their relationships (in cases of non-family groupings); some people will want to bring along information about family history.

Be mindful of the language used to describe the relationships present. The variety of relationships might include long-time neighbors, parent and child/children, spouses, or siblings. The love or bond that is shared can be celebrated without focusing on gender roles or family ties. During introductions, invite each relationship group to describe their relationship and how they choose to refer to themselves. Be sensitive to the presence of same sex couples and the hidden potential for discrimination, since other family groups may include people with a variety of backgrounds. Put special planning into the welcoming language at the beginning of this event, emphasizing that the retreat celebrates all the relationships God has provided.

If there is time, watching the Disney/Pixar movie *Coco* could provide food for thought about the importance of family and how we remain connected to past generations.

Music Resources:

Music can be interspersed throughout the retreat at mealtimes, the beginning and conclusion of group gatherings, and during worship.

Hymns:

- "I Was There To Hear Your Borning Cry" (tune: "Borning Cry"). A poignant retelling of God's love for a beloved child, from birth to death and beyond.

- "When Love Is Found" by Brian Wren (tune: "O Waly Waly"). Although found in the "marriage" section of many hymnals, this familiar tune celebrates the strength of any long-lasting love.

- "Wherever You Go" by Weston Priory/Gregory Norbet. The lyrics of this folk song are taken directly from the book of Ruth. This song is often used in weddings, but since the original biblical text is not about a marital love, the lyrics can apply to any loving relationship.

Songs:

- "All I Ask Of You" by Kathy Zavada. This chant-like song allows listeners to imagine their loved one asking to "forever remember me as loving you."

- "Family Tree" by Tom Chapin. For children and the young-at-heart, a celebration of diversity within families.

- "God Only Knows" by the Beach Boys. A celebration of relationships with a refrain of gratitude.

- "I Will Be Right Here, Waiting For You" by Richard Marx. The Pixar film *Up* celebrates marital love, but the lyrics could also apply to siblings, parent/child, or other relationships.

- "Proud Corazon" by Anthony Gonzalez. This celebratory song from *Coco* describes the impact of family through generations.

- "Round My Family Tree" from *The Tigger Movie*. This fast-paced humorous song lists a variety of relationships that form a family tree.

- "Talking With My Father" by Dougie MacLean. The Scottish singer/songwriter shares poignant memories and thanksgiving for his father.

- "The Family Tree" by Venice. A poignant good-bye to a beloved family member with the recognition of the eternal bonds of family love.

Creating the Atmosphere—Preparing Your Retreat Space:

- Display quote posters you have created.
- Display posters with the names of biblical relationships:
  - Ruth and Naomi (Ruth)
  - Jonathan and David (1 Sam 18)
  - Adam and Eve (Gen 1–2)
  - Abraham and Sarah (Gen 17)
  - Mary and Joseph (Luke 1–2, Matt 1)
  - Andrew and Peter (Matt 4:18)
  - James and John (Mark 10:35–45)
  - Moses, Miriam, and Aaron (Exod 13–15)
  - Joseph and his brothers (Gen 37)
  - Timothy and his grandmother Lois (2 Tim 1)

Worship Area Suggestions:

When creating your altar, consider including these items:

- A branch representing a family tree with the words "family, marriage, friends, siblings, parent, child" hanging from it
- Paper chain with words printed on links: love, loyalty, forever, support, never alone, and so on
- Sign or wooden blocks spelling out "Love" and/or "Family"

Activities and Discussion Questions for Group Gatherings:

These gatherings can be used in any order, depending on the needs of the group and time constraints.

Group Gatherings: We Are All Family

Background:

Before the relationship groups reflect on their shared history, it is important to emphasize the bond that all participants share. As part of the human family, each one created in God's image, we come together as brothers and sisters in God's sight. This activity introduces participants to one another as children of God.

Materials:

Icebreaker activities found in Appendix

Activity:

At the beginning of the retreat and throughout the day, take time to engage the entire group in icebreakers. This will provide participants time to engage with and learn from others in the retreat while encouraging the relationship groups to interact with one another.

Group Gathering: Celebrating Your Story

Background:

This activity introduces the relationship groups to one another.

Materials:

- Cardboard "tents" (6 x 12 inch posterboard folded in half)
- Markers
- Stickers and other craft supplies
- Pictures or mementos participants have brought
- Reflection questions for each group

Activity:

Say to the group:

> There are many kinds of relationships in the world. Some last a lifetime, others for a season. We are born into some of our relationships. Others we seek out and choose for ourselves. All of these relationships enrich our lives and deserve to be celebrated.

Invite each relationship group to decorate one nametag tent. Tell participants:

> Each relationship group will design a nametag for your group. You can include your names and also any title that might describe you (for example: "Solomon Siblings" or "Neighbors and Friends" and so on). You can create your group nametag by using the materials provided.

Bring the whole group together; invite each relationship group to tell their names and relationship. They may also choose to share pictures or mementos.

Group Gathering: Family Tree

Background:

Before the participants discuss their shared relationships, it can be helpful to consider their history. Reflecting on their family trees enables participants to consider influences, heritage, and experiences from the past that they bring to this present-day relationship.

Materials:

- Line drawing of a family tree (can be downloaded online) for each participant or each relationship group (if participants share a family tree)
- Pencils, pens for each participant
- Reflection questions for each relationship group

- Song: "Family Tree" or "Around The Family Tree"

Activity:

Tell the group that they will be talking about family trees. Play the song "Family Tree."

Say to the group:

> The Bible has long lists of descendants that form family trees. This helps establish who a person is and how relationships are interwoven. We will take some time to explore our family trees. Each relationship group will fill out as much as the family tree as possible. If you do not share relatives, you can use the family tree to trace friends, events, or background you may share or have in common.

Allow time for participants to fill out as much of their family tree as possible. Tell them they may enhance their tree by adding any "shrubbery" that might represent close friends or neighbors who were part of their childhood. There may be some "grafted" branches which depict those who became part of the family in a variety of ways.

Family groups change over time and are affected by death, divorce, and other life events. The leader should emphasize the unique nature of each person's family tree; participants may choose how to depict their history by deciding who to include or omit from their family tree.

Encourage each individual to record questions they may have or blanks they wish they could fill in. Direct the groups to engage in conversation with the following questions:

REFLECTION QUESTIONS:

- Which person has been the greatest influence?
- Who is someone you never met, but wish you had?
- List some traits and characteristics found in your family
- What do you bring to new relationships from your family? What do you choose to leave behind?

Invite two to three relationship groups to form a small group to share their family tree. When groups have share, the song "Around The Family Tree" can conclude this gathering.

Group Gathering: How Did We Get Here?

Background:

This activity encourages relationship groups to reminisce as they look back on their shared history. Every relationship has its ups and downs, including moments of closer connection and times when they may be physically absent from one another.

Materials:

- Scroll of paper (at least twelve inches long) for each relationship group
- Markers
- Reflection questions for each relationship group
- Song: "I Will Be Right Here, Waiting For You"

Activity:

Play the song "I Will Be Right Here, Waiting For You." Let the participants know what an accomplishment it is to be on retreat together. They have successfully made time to be together and have made this experience a priority. That is something to celebrate.

Tell the group:

> We are here to appreciate the relationships you share. Now you will create a timeline of your relationship so you can see where you have come from, and perhaps a bit about where you are headed. Include as much detail as possible. There are reflection questions to help you get started, but you can add information that might be unique to your own experience.
>
> Start your timeline with the date your relationship began, and add details by writing or drawing.

- Where and when they met
- Highlights or milestones they have shared together
- Places they have visited together
- Shared acquaintances or family members that enrich their relationship
- What are your hopes and dreams for the future?

Group Gathering: Linked Together

Background:

The people we are closest to often share interests, values, a sense of humor, hobbies, and memories. This activity celebrates the many ways we are connected.

Materials:

- Construction paper strips
- Markers
- Tape
- Song: "Talking With My Father"

Activity:

Tell the group:

> In any relationship, there are many ways that we are connected together. We learn from each other, and that has an influence on who we are. The song "Talking with My Father" is Scottish musician's Dougie MacLean's song of thanksgiving for what he learned from his father.

Play the song; encourage reactions from the group. Engage the group in conversation with the reflection questions.

REFLECTION QUESTIONS:

- The singer talks about the influence of his father and what he has learned from him. Talk about some of the family and friends who have shaped who you are today.

- What do you think make relationships long-lasting?

Tell the group:

> All of you are part of a relationship. This activity gives you the chance to think about what you share together. Read through the reflection questions and answer them together. Then you will create a paper chain as you list the attributes that link you together.

Provide each relationship group with the reflection questions and materials to create a paper chain. Instruct them to record their answers on the paper strips, and then link them together to form a paper chain. The goal is to list as many attributes as possible; the order of the links is not important.

REFLECTION QUESTIONS:

- What do we love about our relationship?
- Shared interests? What are they?
- Shared values? Name some.
- Similar hobbies? What do you like to do together?
- Similar or complimenting personality traits?
- List aspects of your relationship that you cherish.
- Promises you've made to one another

When the groups are finished, invite them to share their chains with the whole group. These can be displayed during the retreat and shared during closing worship.

Group Gathering: Dear Beloved One

Background:

The story of Ruth is an example of a family that was formed by choice. Ruth was married to Naomi's son. Both the son and Naomi's husband died, leaving the women defenseless and alone. Naomi urges Ruth to return to her homeland and her own people, but Ruth refuses, uttering eternal words of love, commitment, and faithfulness. Their story reminds us that the people closest to us may not be related by blood, but may nonetheless form an unshakeable bond.

Materials:

- Copy of Ruth 1:16–17
- Song: "Wherever You Go"
- Stationary or greeting cards
- Pens

Activity:

Say to the group:

> We will hear a story of a famous biblical relationship. What is remarkable about this relationship is that the two women—Ruth and Naomi—were not related to each other. Naomi is Ruth's mother-in-law. But Ruth pledges an undying love to her that is inspirational to any kind of relationship.

Read Ruth 1:16–17 to the group.
Play the song "Wherever You Go," which is inspired by the story of Ruth.

Say to the group:

> We may not always take the time to express the importance another person has to us. We may not be as eloquent as Ruth; our words may seem inadequate, or may be difficult to voice.
>
> We are going to take the time to write a letter to the person (people) who came with us on this retreat. Think about what you would like them to know. Some things you might want to share with them:
>
> - Why you are glad they are here
>
> - Something you appreciate about them
>
> - Thankfulness for something they did or said
>
> Your letter doesn't need to be long, but it gives you the opportunity to share your feelings with this special person.

Encourage participants to take enough time to write (or draw) a thoughtful message to those in their relationship group. When they have completed their messages, invite them to share those within their relationship group.

Play the song "Wherever You Go" again to close this gathering.

Crafting Our Message: Circles of Love

Purpose:

Create a collage representing valued relationships

Materials:

- Sixteen-inch cardboard circles (try obtaining from local pizza shop). Make a small hole so craft can be hung up when completed

- Ribbon (for hanging up craft)

- Magazines

- Scissors

- Paper

- Glue
- Markers

DIRECTIONS:

Encourage participants to think about the many relationships in their lives. These may include people from family, work, church, neighborhoods, and so on.

Tell participants to draw a circle in the center of the cardboard that represents them. Then create a collage honoring the important relationships in your life. These may be formed in concentric circles, as "pie pieces," jigsaw puzzle fashion, or any way they choose.

Instruct participants to cut out pictures and words from the magazines; these will be glued onto the circle to create the collage. They may also write words or quotes to be added to the collage.

When participants have completed their craft, invite them to talk about their collages. These may be added to the worship area as a celebration of the relationships that enrich their lives.

Worship Resources:

These are themed resources to go with this particular retreat. Additional resources are available in the Appendix.

Litanies

> Leader: Loving God, you know us and promise your faithfulness.
>
> People: No matter who we are or where we are on life's journey, you welcome us.
>
> Leader: You have established a covenant with us.
>
> People: Wherever we go, you go with us. Wherever we live, you are there.
>
> Leader: We can depend on your steadfast love.
>
> People: We rely on your words, "I will never leave you or forsake you."

Leader: God of yesterday, of precious memories, of times gone but cherished.

People: Thank you for special moments shared. Let us remember and give thanks.

Leader: God of today, of hospitality and welcome, of time set aside to just be.

People: Thank you for these moments of retreat that we share with cherished ones.

Leader: God of tomorrow, of what will yet be, unknown to us, but we are safe in your care.

People: Thank you for companions on the journey, for your love made apparent through others. For the gift of love, for the gift of time, for the gift of presence, we give you thanks.

Unison Prayer (inspired by 1 Cor 13)

God of love, we celebrate loving relationships, people who want the best for us. We marvel at the ones who always have time for us, people we can call any time of day or night. We rejoice in comfortable relationships where explanations aren't necessary and a listening ear is always available. Help us to be givers and receivers of love. Remind us to be patient and kind. Help us not be rude or pushy, but to be compassionate and caring. Let us share the gift of bearing, believing, hoping, and enduring all things—with and for one another. We can love because you first loved us. Thank you. Amen.

Candle-Lighting

Participants can be invited to remember or honor family or friends who have died but are still influential in their lives. Provide votive candles (either electric or traditional) and invite participants to name those cherished people.

They may choose to say one of the following:

- I remember and give thanks for _____.
- My life is better because of _____.
- I carry the memory of _____ within me.

Chapter 11

Experiencing Wilderness

Friends on the Journey through Challenging Times

About This Theme:

Sometimes our lives run smoothly; we make a plan, execute it, and the details fall into place. This might be called a "green pasture" time, where our lives proceed with little disruption or upset.

There are, however, other seasons. Plans fall apart, roadblocks obstruct our progress, friends or family let us down, or the unexpected happens and the bottom drops out of our orderly world. Suddenly nothing makes sense, and the way forward seems impossible or unclear. This is "wilderness."

Although it would be natural to avoid these trying times, biblical stories demonstrate wilderness as a part of the human experience. This retreat helps participants gain perspective on their wilderness experience. Whether they are struggling with personal challenges or delivering aid as caretakers, this retreat offers supportive encouragement. This time of respite and renewal provides a new appreciation of God's promise to provide strength for the journey.

Scripture Focus:

- Exodus 3:1–12

- Exodus 13:17–18, 20–22
    - Exodus 14:10–13, 21–25
    - Exodus 15:20–22
    - Exodus 16:4–5

"Quotable":

- "God led the people by the roundabout way of the wilderness toward the Red Sea" (Exod 13:18).
- "The Lord went in front of them in a pillar of cloud by day, to lead them along the way, and in a pillar of fire by night" (Exod 13:21).
- "Be strong and courageous; do not be frightened or dismayed, for the Lord your God is with you wherever you go" (Josh 1:9).
- "Do not fear, for I am with you, do not be afraid, for I am your God" (Isa 41:10).
- "I am with you always, to the end of the age" (Matt 28:20).
- "In the midst of every difficulty lies an opportunity."—Albert Einstein.

Introductory Objects and Bring-Along Items:

Invite participants to bring an object that represents where they are on their life's journey. Encourage them to consider what might symbolize how their daily time or efforts are spent, either at home or work.

Encourage participants to bring poems, quotes, readings, or songs that relate to theme; these can be shared during worship and group gatherings.

Crowdsource materials for the craft activity; in particular, encourage participants to bring old shoes that they no longer want.

Leader's Tip:

A wooden or paper finger labyrinth can be a useful tool to describe a journey. By demonstrating the labyrinth's path to the center, you can reflect on the twists and turns of life. Unlike a maze, the final destination of a labyrinth is never in question; the length of the journey is the only variable.

The traveler may choose or be compelled to linger along the way, which reminds us that our path is rarely without detours.

For centuries, Christians have walked on labyrinths outdoors or inside cathedrals to meditate on their spiritual journey. The winding path can remind us that, whether our journey leads us by still waters, through dark valleys, or to green pastures, God's presence is assured.

As leader, you can demonstrate a finger labyrinth as an introduction to the theme of walking in the wilderness. Extensive information about labyrinths is available from the Labyrinth Society (labyrinthsociety.org) and on wikiHow (wikihow.com). You may also provide copies of finger labyrinths (found online) to participants for their own prayer and reflection.

If there is time, you might choose to show the movie *Wild*. If any participants enjoy camping or hiking, you may wish to invite them to reflect on positive experiences in wilderness.

Music Resources:

Music can be interspersed throughout the retreat at mealtimes, the beginning and conclusion of group gatherings, and during worship.

Hymns:

- "The Care The Eagle Gives Her Young" (tune: "Crimond"). Particularly appropriate for caregivers supporting those in the "wilderness."

- "Glory, Glory Hallelujah" (tune: "Glory, Glory"). A song of celebration and hope that encourages listeners to "lay our burdens down" and receive God's help and support.

- "Guide Me, O My Great Redeemer" (tune: "Cwm Rhondda"). A prayer for guidance in times of confusion; this song draws on the images of the people of Israel wandering in the wilderness.

- "In The Midst Of New Dimensions" (tune: "New Dimensions"). This rousing hymn praises God's guidance as we face an unknown future.

- "When Israel Was In Egypt's Land" (tune: "Go Down, Moses"). This heartfelt African-American spiritual recounts the pain of captivity and joy of release.

- "We Are Marching In The Light of God" (tune: "Siyahamba"). A South African protest song calls for freedom to celebrate God's light, power, and love. The lively rhythm can inspire us to march—or dance!

Songs:

- "Climb Every Mountain" by Rodgers and Hammerstein. Audra McDonald, Christina Aguilera, and the Mormon Tabernacle Choir are among the many artists who sing this inspirational song about confronting obstacles.
- "Follow The Drinking Gourd." A moving description of slaves' journey to freedom, following the light of the North Star found in the Drinking Gourd (Big Dipper).
- "Just Around The Riverbend" by Alan Menken. This lyrical song from the movie *Pocahontas* describes exploring life's twists and turns.
- "Traveling In The Wilderness" by John McCutcheon. Harriet Tubman and Frederick Douglass are among the examples of those who braved hardships to travel to the Promised Land.
- "Sanctuary" by Carrie Newcomer. This lovely song recognizes the life-giving moments of rest and renewal needed along the journey.
- "You'll Never Walk Alone" by Rodgers and Hammerstein. Susan Boyle, Josh Groban, Elvis Presley, and Gerry and the Pacemakers offer interpretations of this stirring song.

Creating the Atmosphere—Preparing Your Retreat Space:

- Display your retreat schedule in several places
- Scatter road signs around: "One Way," "Do Not Enter," "U-Turn," "Stop," "Danger," and so on
- Display quotes

Worship Area Suggestions:

When creating an altar, you might include these items:

- Finger labyrinth
- Hiking boots
- Walking sticks, cane, and/or walker
- Map
- Compass
- Sextant

Activities and Discussion Questions for Group Gatherings:

These gatherings can be used in any order, depending on the needs of the group and time constraints.

Group Gathering: What is Wilderness?

Background:

Participants will brainstorm a definition of wilderness. Because this experience is different for everyone, there may be a wide variety of answers. Encourage the group to thoughtfully consider all responses as they are shared and recorded.

Remind the group of the story of the people of Israel, who had been enslaved for hundreds of years. Finally, they are going to be released from captivity. Rather than lead them directly to freedom and the Promised Land, God allows them to wander "by the roundabout way of the wilderness" (Exod 13:17).

Materials:

- Newsprint entitled, "Wilderness"
- Marker
- Copy of Exodus 13:17–18, 20–22
- Pictures of wilderness

Activity:

Tell the group:

> We will be looking at pictures of wilderness and hearing about the experience of the people of Israel, who spent forty years wandering in the wilderness on their way to the Promised Land. Then we will come up with a definition of what wilderness is.

Invite a volunteer to read Exodus 13: 17–18, 20–22 out loud.

Show participants a variety of images of wilderness one at a time. Invite participants to respond by offering words or phrases to describe the experience of wilderness. Enlist a volunteer to record responses. When everyone has had an opportunity to speak, ask the group to reflect on the words. You can lead a short conversation with some of these questions:

REFLECTION QUESTIONS:

- What similarities do you see in these words?
- What differences are there? Why do you think that is?
- Is wilderness always a negative experience? When could it be positive?
- Do some people permanently dwell in wilderness? If so, what might that be like?

Tell the group it is now time to create a group definition for the word "wilderness." Ask them to fill in the blank, "Wilderness is _____." This conversation may take some time and negotiation as the group establishes a consensus on the feelings and experience of wilderness.

The group may discover both positive and negative definitions for the experience of wilderness. Listen carefully to the group and be willing to add/subtract words and phrases to develop a definition.

Group Gathering: What Does Wilderness Look Like?

Background:

Everyone might have a variety of ideas of what wilderness looks like. This activity allows participants to brainstorm and develop a physical representation of wilderness. This can broaden their definition of wilderness and its impact on life.

Materials:

Bag for each small group containing a variety of building materials. Each bag can contain different materials and might include Legos, Lincoln Logs, wooden blocks, sticks, stones, leaves, grasses, crumpled paper, onion peels, a tin can, and so on. Each group should also receive a plate or piece of cardboard on which to build their structure.

Activity:

Divide the group into teams of three to four people. Give each team a bag with materials listed above. Tell them:

> You will have twenty minutes to create a visual image of wilderness. Since this is your interpretation, there are no right or wrong answers. Before you start to build, talk about what a wilderness might look or feel like. Use those ideas to construct your symbol. You can use some or all of the materials in the bag, plus any others you can find. Your creation can be two- or three-dimensional, and it can be large or small.

Music can be played in the background as the groups use their imaginations to create an image of wilderness. This light-hearted exercise may also invite participants into thoughtful reflection. It provides a safe environment for participants to share some initial thoughts about the experience of wilderness.

When the time is up (the groups may never feel completely done, but assure them that whatever they have to share will be interesting to others), bring the group back together. Invite each small group to describe and talk about their creation.

These images of wilderness may be added to your worship center or displayed in a place where participants can examine them during the retreat.

Group Gathering: Who is Your Moses?

Background:

This activity encourages participants to consider who has offered support during their wilderness times. In the book of Exodus, the people of Israel had toiled in slavery for centuries until God sent Moses to guide them to freedom. In the same way, Harriet Tubman led American slaves to freedom in Canada, earning her the nickname "Moses." The song "Follow The Drinking Gourd" refers to the fugitives relying on the stars in the Drinking Gourd, also known as the Big Dipper, to guide them north.

Materials:

- Blindfold for each participant
- Songs: "Follow The Drinking Gourd" and "Traveling In The Wilderness"
- Copy of Exodus 3:7–12
- Arrow-shaped pieces of posterboard, six to eight inches long, for each participant
- Markers

Activity:

Tell participants:

> Sometimes it is impossible to escape the wilderness without help. Harriet Tubman led approximately three hundred slaves to freedom. Her nickname was "Moses" as she led captives to the "Promised Land" of Canada and freedom.

Play the song "Follow The Drinking Gourd."

Invite a volunteer to read Exodus 3:7–12.

> God called Moses to lead the people of Israel out of bondage to the Promised Land of Israel. We are going to experience what it means to trust someone to lead us safely.

Tell the group to count off by twos in order to form pairs with the person next to them. Explain that this next activity allows everyone to have the chance to experience what it is like to need a Moses, or a guide.

Instruct everyone to put on a blindfold. Tell the group:

> If I told everyone to get up and walk across the room with your blindfolds on, what would happen?

Leave time for responses. Then say:

> Clearly, you need a guide in order to stay safe. All the people who had the number one, leave your blindfold on. Everyone who was a number two, remove your blindfold—you are now a guide.

Tell each guide to choose a destination within the building to lead their partner. Encourage the pairs to communicate clearly with their partners. They should ask questions to understand the needs of their partner before they start moving.

Tell the group:

> The guide is responsible for the safety of the other person. Be sure to give that person clear instructions about when to turn and what to avoid. The guides must also listen carefully to the needs of their partner. When you have reached your location, switch places so the guide will become the follower. Everyone should return back to this location together.

When the group has re-assembled, engage them in conversation with these questions:

Reflection Questions:

- How did it feel to be blindfolded? To be led?
- Describe the experience of being responsible for someone else and leading that person.
- Did you prefer being a guide or a follower? Why?
- What does this experience tell us about times when we find ourselves in the wilderness?

Invite the group to consider people who guided them through wilderness moments of their lives. Encourage them to take a few moments to think about those who have offered support and guidance.

Tell them:

> A wilderness experience can be made easier when we have someone who acts as our "Moses" or "Harriet Tubman." We may not always appreciate or be aware of those guides until we have emerged from the wilderness and can look back to gain perspective.

Provide each participant with a posterboard arrow. Invite them to give thanks for those who have offered them direction and support in their lives by writing the names of those people who pointed them in the right direction. They may also choose to add a short note of appreciation to those listed on their arrows.

Invite the group to briefly share about those named on their arrows. The arrows can be hung up or added to the worship area.

Listen to "Traveling In The Wilderness" to close this gathering.

Group Gathering: Singing Songs of Freedom

Background:

When the people of Israel finally cross the Red Sea into freedom, Moses' sister Miriam leads the people in a song of victory. They have escaped slavery! Their joy is overwhelming; although they are not yet in the Promised Land, they dance and sing praises to God.

Materials:

- Copy of Exodus 15:20–22 for each participant
- Newsprint and marker
- Paper and pen for each participant

Activity:

Ask a volunteer to read Exodus 15:20–22 out loud. Ask the group to list the emotions of someone who has broken free from a wilderness experience and is just beginning to feel the joy of freedom. Record those emotions on newsprint.

Tell them:

> Now it is your turn to write a short song of joy and thanksgiving. Take a familiar tune like "Row, Row, Row Your Boat," "Twinkle, Twinkle Little Star," or another song and put new words to it. Remember Miriam's song and imagine you are adding verses to it. Think about how you would express your gratitude at being released from a time of captivity or wilderness.

Divide into small groups to brainstorm song lyrics. Remind participants that the song is not meant to be a masterpiece, but rather a heartfelt expression of freedom.

Encourage participants to share their completed songs, and perhaps to sing some of them during worship.

Group Gathering: Mapping our Journeys

Background:

When Moses led the people of Israel through the wilderness, they did not experience a straight path or an easy route. Often, they were not where they wanted to be, but they discovered God was with them. Often, they did not have everything they desired, but they discovered that God provided them with enough.

Materials:

- Pictures of winding rivers
- Pieces of newsprint or butcher-block paper (three feet long) for each participant
- Markers, colored pencils
- Newsprint with list of questions
- Copy of Exodus 13:17–18, 21–22; 16:4–5
- Songs: "Just Around The River Bend," "You Will Never Walk Alone"

Activity:

This activity allows participants to reflect on their own journeys and experience with wilderness. Tell the group to consider some of their life's joys and challenges.

Tell the group that the Exodus story details the twists and turns of the former slaves' journey. Invite three volunteers to read Exodus 13:17–18, 21–22, and Exodus 16:4–5.

Tell participants:

> It was a long trip between captivity and entering the Promised Land. Along the way, the people encountered God in unexpected ways. God provided manna as well as a cloud and a pillar of fire to guide them. We are going to reflect on our journey and consider where and how we have encountered God along the way.

Explain to the group that they will be using the image of a river as a metaphor for their life journey. Say:

> Our lives might be visualized as a river flowing through the landscape. Some rivers flow in a straight line with a swiftly-moving current, but most have twists and turns along the way.

Invite them to listen to the song "Just Around The Riverbend," which describes a river changing and going in different directions. The listener is encouraged to be open to life's movement and whatever may be coming next. Tell them:

> A river may have sections where it is flowing freely and other areas where there are obstructions or dams. These may be times of wilderness, when our path has not been moving forward easily.
>
> There may be a series of eddies, where water swirls around and around, which can make us wonder if we will make any progress. Rivers can contain large oxbows that can slow down the current—this might be a welcome respite from periods of whitewater, or may be experienced as a frustrating pause in forward motion.

Explain to the group that everyone will draw their journey, using a river as an image. Remind them that artistic skills are not necessary; the markers or colored pencils are being used as tools to reflect on their "river of life."

As they prepare to draw their river, ask the participants to consider these questions:

- Where did your river start?
- Has there been any rough water along the way?
- Have you encountered obstructions or wilderness?
- Is your river meandering or moving quickly?
- Have there been eddies or times when you've gotten caught up in the bushes?
- What is the scenery like? What have you seen along the way?
- Are you alone on your river? Has anyone traveled part of the way with you?

Provide each participant with a large sheet of newsprint and access to markers and/or colored pencils in a variety of colors.

Explain that no one will be able to draw an entire life story, but everyone is invited to depict highlights or important events along the way.

Allow participants enough time to map out their journey and add as much detail as possible (usually at least thirty minutes). When participants have reached a stopping point, form small groups so they may talk about their journeys and experiences of wilderness. If possible, display the participants' rivers of life on the wall or on tables.

Invite the group to listen to the song "You Will Never Walk Alone" to close the gathering.

Group Gathering: Addressing Our Wilderness

Background:

This empowering exercise allows participants to address their wilderness directly. We often talk about our struggles, but rarely do we address them directly. As leader, you may choose to provide a variety of materials to enable participants to communicate with a challenge they or a loved one are facing. You may also choose to provide notecards and envelopes so participants may literally write a letter to their wilderness. These could be collected and mailed to the participants in a few weeks.

Materials:

- Paper and pen
- Construction paper
- Markers
- Colored pencils
- Stickers
- Magazines, calendar pages
- Glue

Activity:

Invite participants to imagine that they can speak directly to a challenge they are facing. Encourage them to consider what they would like to say.

Imagine what it would be like to write letters such as these: "Dear Cancer"; "To: Alcohol, From: Recovering One"; or "Attention: Fear."

The wilderness can be addressed literally with a letter or through a hands-on activity such as creating a collage, illustrating a picture, or drawing a map. Since this is an exercise of imagination, any form of expression is welcome.

Provide the group with some questions to consider as they address their wilderness. These may be posted on newsprint or read out loud:

- When do you feel most supported in your wilderness?
- When did you feel most alone? What would have helped you?
- What scared you?
- What were you sure of?
- What did you doubt?

Say to the group:

> This may only be the beginning of your conversation. You will bring your letter/craft home with you; you may want to add to it as time goes by.

When the group has completed their project, invite them to describe the experience to the group. Some people may choose to share their creation at closing worship.

Crafting Our Message: Walk in My Shoes

Purpose:

The expression "don't judge people until you have walked a mile in their shoes" takes on new meaning with this activity. By re-imagining and re-purposing shoes, participants creatively express their experience of wilderness.

Note: This craft can be completed in less than two hours; alternatively, it can be expanded to include significant amounts of time both for creating and for reflecting on the meaning of the creations. This activity encourages a sense of empathy and curiosity about one another's journey as we try to imagine walking in one another's shoes.

Materials:

- Shoes of every type: sandals, sneakers, heels, children's, men's and women's, slippers, and so on
- Glue guns
- Sharp scissors
- Paintbrushes
- Variety of craft materials including (but not limited to) yarn, magazines, tissue paper, paint, or glitter
- Outline of a footprint for each participant
- Optional: music

Directions:

Tell the group that if shoes could talk, they could tell much of our story. We usually wear shoes, so they go with us when we are walking toward a destination, dragging our feet toward an unwanted destination, skipping with joy, or standing still because we are immobilized or don't know the way forward.

Shoes can help describe our wilderness walking experience.

Tell the group:

> We will use these shoes to express our wilderness experience. Think about where you are on your journey and what that experience is like. Look over the shoes and see what might represent your experience. If you are feeling wobbly right now, you may choose a high heel shoe. If you are filled with child-like joy or are wishing someone could just take care of you, you might select a child's shoe.
>
> Once you choose a shoe, you will decorate it. There are two options about how to use your shoe:
>
> - Your shoe can represent a wilderness you are experiencing now.
> - Your shoe can represent the direction you hope to be heading.

Each participant will choose a shoe. Explain that they will transform the shoe with the craft materials available; they are free to cut, break, decorate, or change the shoe in any way they choose.

Allow at least an hour for shoe-decorating. As participants finish, invite them to complete this sentence on the provided paper "footprint:" "If you were to walk a day in my shoes . . ." Encourage participants to write as much as they are willing about what their re-purposed shoe means and how it expresses their wilderness experience.

The completed shoes can become part of the worship area or can be displayed along a hallway or sidewalk with the footprints so participants can consider what it means to walk in another person's wilderness.

Worship Resources:

These are themed resources to go with this particular retreat. Additional resources are available in the Appendix.

Litanies:

Leader: God of the wilderness, guide me in my wandering.

People: When I reach Red Sea dead ends, help me trust you to lead me through.

Leader: Split open my doubt, reveal an unexpected pathway.

People: Help me go forward by faith, one step at a time.

Leader: Labyrinth God, twisting and weaving through my life, help me trust your path.

People: God of the burning bush, open my eyes and spirit to your wonders.

Leader: Pillar of fire, lead me to your light.

People: Pillar of cloud, envelop me with your grace.

Leader: The journey is long; my faith is not always strong.

People: The journey is long; your faithfulness is always sure.

Unison Prayer

Guide of my life, I prefer green pastures. If I were going to pre-book this trip, I would reserve a lifetime of still waters with glorious views of sunlit mountains and wildflower-filled meadows. My meals would be banquets highlighted by cups overflowing with abundance. Apparently, I am on a different voyage. When I wander alone and afraid in dark valleys, reassure me. When enemies and evil-doers frighten me, help me recognize your guidance, which comforts me. Surely, your goodness is with me. Now and forever. Amen.

Chapter 12

Practicing Daily Gratitude
Developing Awareness of God's Blessings

About This Theme:

This retreat celebrates the life-giving discipline of gratitude and giving thanks. Gratitude does not ignore concerns or pretend that everything is "just fine." Gratitude encourages us to recognize God's presence in the midst of life's ups and downs. Giving thanks does not negate difficult situations or minimalize challenging circumstances. Instead, it raises awareness of God's tenacious faithfulness and celebrates God's loving support.

Psalm 23 assures that God accompanies us in both peaceful green valleys and in the darkest shadows. We may not give thanks for all circumstances, but we can give thanks in them, and discover more about God in the process. Praising God can become a powerful daily ritual that enriches our lives and increases our consciousness of God's presence. This retreat immerses participants in the experience of giving thanks and offers practical tools to develop a gratitude prayer practice at home.

Scripture Focus:

- Psalm 23
- Psalm 92:1–4
- Psalm 117

- Habakkuk 3:17–18
- Colossians 3:14–17
- 1 Thessalonians 5: 13–18

"Quotable":

- Psalm 117 in several translations
- "Though the fig tree does not blossom . . . yet I will rejoice in the Lord" (Hab 3:17–18).
- "It is good to give thanks to the Lord" (Ps 92:1).
- "Be thankful. Let the word of Christ dwell in you richly" (Col 3:16).
- "Rejoice always. Pray without ceasing. Give thanks in all circumstances" (1 Thess 5:16–18).
- "If the only prayer you pray in your life is 'thank you,' that would suffice."—Meister Eckhart
- "I am not discouraged, for every wrong attempt discarded is another step forward."—Thomas Alva Edison
- "Cultivate the habit of being grateful for every good thing that comes to you, and to give thanks continuously. And because all things have contributed to your advancement, you should include all things in your gratitude."—Ralph Waldo Emerson
- "Do not spoil what you have by desiring what you have not; remember that what you now have was once among the things you only hoped for."—Epicurus
- "I look up at the blue sky and the bare chestnut tree, on whose branches little raindrops shine, appearing like silver, and at the seagulls and other birds as they glide on the wind. As long as this exists . . . and I may live to see it, this sunshine, these cloudless skies, while this lasts I cannot be unhappy."—Anne Frank

Introductory Objects and Bring-Along Items:

Invite participants to bring an object or picture to represent something that fills them with gratitude. One caveat: no family pictures! Although many (most?) people are grateful for their families, this retreat encourages participants to dig deeper and move beyond the easiest and most obvious answers. Encourage participants to think outside the box as they consider their blessings.

In addition, encourage participants to bring quotes, short poems, or Scripture verses related to this theme to share during worship and group gatherings. This can be an engaging way to both learn more about one another and expand the repertoire of readings and songs during the retreat.

Leader's Tip:

In the days or weeks leading up to the retreat, take a few moments each day to intentionally cultivate your own gratitude practice. List three blessings daily in a simple gratitude journal. By developing gratitude in your own life, you will be better prepared to encourage participants to explore the rich blessings of giving thanks.

Brother David Steindl-Rast's website, "www.gratefulness.org," is a wonderful resource for helpful insights about gratitude.

Additional Resources:

Beautifully illustrated children's books based on gratitude hymns could be added to the book nook or shared during worship:

- *God of the Sparrow, God of the Whale* by Jaroslav J. Vayda (New York: Church, 2001).

- *For the Beauty of the Earth* by Folliot S. Pierpoint (Minneapolis: Sparkhouse, 2017).

Music Resources:

Music can be interspersed throughout the retreat at mealtimes, the beginning and conclusion of group gatherings, and during worship.

Hymns:

- "Come, You Thankful People Come" (tune: "St. George's Windsor"). This invitational hymn compels listeners to offer praise to God.

- "For The Beauty Of The Earth" (tune: "Dix"). Singers can reflect on their blessings as each verse joyfully concludes, "Lord of all to thee we raise, this our hymn of grateful praise!"

- "God Of The Sparrow, God Of The Whale" (tune: "Roeder"). A singable hymn that inspires awe at God's bountiful gifts.

- "Great Is Your Faithfulness" (tune: "Faithfulness"). A profound celebration of God's generosity and grace.

- "It Is Well With My Soul" (tune: "Ville du Havre"). Poignant statement of thanks following tragic loss.

- "Now Thank We All Our God" (tune: "Nun Danket"). Written during the Thirty Years' War, this hymn encourages praise even in dire circumstances.

Songs:

- "All Good Gifts" by Stephen Schwartz (from the musical "Godspell"). Inspired by Psalm 100, this song joyfully invites listeners to "thank the Lord." Several beautiful video versions are available on YouTube.

- "Everything Is Holy Now" by Peter Mayer. Gratitude for gifts large and small is celebrated because "everything is holy now."

- "For The Beauty Of The Earth" by John Rutter. This stirring anthem offers a fresh, uplifting version of the familiar hymn. Stunning photographs accompany the music on YouTube.

- "I Believe" by Carrie Newcomer. A down-to-earth list of homey experiences that are both life-changing and affirming.

- "My Favorite Things" by Rodgers and Hammerstein. This much-loved song from *The Sound of Music* emphasizes gratitude in times of fear or sadness.

- "My Tribute" by Andraé Crouch. Humbled by God's many gifts, Crouch wonders, "how can I say thanks?"

- "Psalm 117" by Seven Places. This song beautifully conveys the power of praising God. YouTube version offers stunning graphics.
- "What a Wonderful World" by Louis Armstrong. Many YouTube videos with beautiful images accompany this classic song or simply enjoy listening to gratitude expressed.

Creating the Atmosphere—Preparing Your Retreat Space:

- Display the schedule for your retreat in several places so it is easily seen by participants.
- Display posters with quotes that you have made.
- Prepare sheets of newsprint as public gratitude journals. At the top of each page, write a sentence and invite participants to respond with gratitude. Some examples might be:
- I give thanks for beloved pets:
- I give thanks for mentors/people I have learned from:
- I give thanks for beautiful places:
- I give thanks for acts of kindness:
- I give thanks for people who makes me laugh:
- I give thanks for . . .

Provide markers by each piece of newsprint so participants can write or draw their responses.

Worship Area Suggestions:

When creating a worship area, consider including these items:

- Symbols of bounty: baskets or bowls filled with fruit, a fountain to represent overflowing cups
- Flowers
- Cornucopia

Activities and Discussion Questions for Group Gatherings:

These gatherings can be used in any order, depending on the group's needs and time constraints.

Group Gathering: What Does Gratitude Look Like?

Background:

As participants reflect on the importance of giving thanks, they will create a symbolic expression of gratitude. Psalm 117, the shortest psalm in the Bible, offers the inspiration for this exercise. This doxology, or song of praise, exhorts listeners to give thanks and praise God.

The materials used in the activity do not need to be purchased; part of the exercise is using available materials to express our gratitude.

Materials:

- Song: "Psalm 117"
- Psalm 117 in several translations
- A wide variety of supplies can be used in creating a symbol of gratitude. Place objects in a bag or box for each small group; offering a variety of objects for each group will result in diverse expressions of gratitude. Some examples might include:
- Pitcher
- Bowls of various sizes
- Baskets
- Water
- Rice or other grains
- Crepe paper
- Tissue paper
- Glue
- Leaves, grasses, branches
- Markers, crayons, colored pencils

- Scissors
- Old greeting cards

Activity:

Tell the group:

> We will listen to several different versions of Psalm 117, which is the shortest psalm in the Bible. This psalm is an invitation to give thanks to God. In just a few lines, the psalmist does two things: they tell people to praise God and they tell people why they should—because God is faithful. First, we will listen to a musical version of the psalm, then we will hear different translations of the psalm.

Play the song "Psalm 117."

Invite participants to read translations of Psalm 117 to the group.

Engage the group in conversation with these questions:

REFLECTION QUESTIONS:

- Why do you think the psalmist tells people to praise God?
- Why is praising God a good thing to do?
- Why does God deserve to be praised?

  Form groups of three to four people. Tell the groups:

> You have the opportunity to create a visual expression of gratitude. What do you think gratitude looks like? You can use any of the supplies provided and any additional materials/objects you can find. Use your imaginations to create a symbol of gratitude. After you have created your symbol, give it a caption or a title by using a quote, Scripture, or your own words.

This light-hearted activity allows participants to brainstorm together and creatively express themselves. Once their creations are complete, each group can present their creation with an explanation.

These symbols can be placed in the worship/altar area, or otherwise put on display as inspiration.

Group Gathering: Personal Gratitude Calendars

Background:

The act of intentionally giving thanks can make us aware of blessings in our lives. Sometimes we take these for granted or overlook them. The act of recording them daily can enhance our powers of observation and increase our awareness of God's gifts.

Materials:

- Song or hymn of your choice
- Psalm 92:1–4
- Calendar page for current month for each participant
- Pen for each person
- Discussion questions for each person

Activity:

Invite a volunteer to read Psalm 92:1–4; explain that the psalm tells us, "It is good to give thanks to the Lord" (verse 1).

Listen or sing one of the listed songs or hymns.

Tell the group:

> Think about the blessings in your life. Consider people, experiences, places and activities that enrich your life.
>
> We are going to consider our blessings by creating a prayer calendar. Look for today's date and write three to five blessings in that calendar square. There isn't much room to write! Just jot down a word or two for each.
>
> Then think about yesterday and write three to five blessings you experienced. Try to think beyond the obvious ones, which might be your family, friends, or home. Go a bit

deeper and consider other aspects of your life that make you grateful. Blessings may be large or small. They might include:

- Sunlight filtering through the window
- A good night's sleep
- An anticipated visit or event
- Hearing a child laugh

The calendar spaces are deliberately small so you won't feel overwhelmed by the thought of recording blessings every day. Write as much as you can.

When everyone has filled two calendar squares, divide into smaller groups (two to four people each) and invite them to discuss the reflection questions.

Discussion Questions:

- What are your blessings for today?
- What were your blessings yesterday?
- What is the benefit of giving thanks every day?
- What prevents us from doing that?
- Would our lives change if we gave thanks for "everyday" blessings such as clean water, enough food, shoes, and a place to sleep?

When everyone has had an opportunity to speak, bring the group back together and ask for comments or observations.

Encourage participants to take the calendar page home with them and consider making this part of a daily gratitude practice. They could use a calendar at home to daily jot down blessings they have experienced. This intentional awareness can help develop a practice of gratitude.

Play or sing a song to conclude this gathering time.

Group Gathering: Haiku of Gratitude

Background:

By using the poetic form of haiku, participants can observe beauty around them and express their thanks.

Materials:

- Pen and paper for each participant
- Newsprint with the haiku pattern written out (see example below)
- Newsprint with haiku examples
- Newsprint and marker to create group haikus

Activity:

Explain to the group that a haiku is a traditional Japanese poem which has three lines with the following haiku pattern:

- five syllables
- seven syllables
- five syllables

The brevity of the poem makes it accessible even to those with no writing or poetry experience. It does not rhyme, but uses often simple words to describe what is being seen or experienced.

Explain the haiku pattern to the group. Tell the group:

> A haiku encourages a writer to express a description or feeling with just a few words. A haiku encourages us to pay attention to what we see, feel, and hear so we can capture that experience in a short, but powerful poem.
>
> This is not about creating a perfect poem, but about attuning our senses to the beauty around us. We attempt to capture that experience with our words, using this form.

Read these haiku examples (or others that you have found):

I welcome springtime
Green, fresh, new life, revival
Speaks to my spirit.

Gently lapping waves
Quacking ducks glide gently by
Beauty in a pond.

These short poems offer images that help us envision a scene ("Apple blossoms bloom"). Haikus can also compel listeners to imagine sounds ("Wild geese honking overhead") or people ("Wobbly toddler climbs"). With just a few short lines, a haiku can create an image for the listener or engage many of the senses.

Before participants try composing their own haikus, invite them to practice by writing several five-syllable lines as a group. This will help those who may be hesitant to experiment with the haiku form.

Ask these questions as a writing prompt to help the group to help identify a topic or idea for the group haiku:

QUESTIONS:

- What are you grateful for right now?
- Fill in the blank, "Today I give thanks for _____."
- How are you feeling right now on retreat? Let's see if we can come up with words to describe these feelings.

Invite participants to suggest some five-syllable lines. Have the group work together to brainstorm some potential first lines of a haiku. Write down as many as possible to help the group become comfortable with the form. Record these on newsprint as examples to inspire participants when they are writing individual haikus.

Take time to enjoy the process of writing a group haiku. Having a sense of humor while writing can enhance the process of counting syllables and discovering descriptive words.

When several examples are recorded, encourage participants to write their own haikus. Some people might write several, while others will use the time to craft a single poem. Encourage them by saying:

> Now it's your turn. Take a moment to get inspiration for your haiku. You can write haikus to express gratitude for retreat time, for people in your lives, cherished memories, the beauty around you, whatever you wish. You may write one or several.

Allow enough time (twenty to thirty minutes) for writing. When participants are ready, invite them to reflect on the experience and to share their haikus, as desired. Encourage participants to continue to experiment with this writing form as the retreat continues.

The haikus can be read as part of closing worship.

Group Gathering: Giving Thanks in Challenging Times

Background:

Even in good times, we may forget to appreciate our blessings or neglect to offer praise and thanksgiving. When tragedy enters our lives, all thoughts of gratitude and praise can completely disappear. This activity encourages us to consider how to seek God's presence in the midst of despair and to give thanks for God's support.

Depending on the group and the length or depth of conversation, you may wish to plan a break partway through this gathering.

Materials:

- Pens
- Paper
- Recording: "It Is Well With My Soul"
- Lyrics: "It Is Well With My Soul"
- Guidelines for writing a prayer for each participant

Display these quotes:

- "Though the fig tree does not blossom . . . yet I will rejoice in the Lord" (Hab 3:17–18)

- "I am not discouraged, for every wrong attempt discarded is another step forward."—Thomas Alva Edison

- "If the only prayer you pray in your life is 'thank you,' that would suffice."—Meister Eckhart

Activity:

Read the quotes out loud one a time. Invite the group into conversation with these questions:

REFLECTION QUESTIONS:

- What is your reaction to these quotes?

- Does one appeal to you more than another?

- Do you agree or disagree with them?

- The job of a fig tree is to produce fruit. When it fails to do that, the farmer suffers great loss. What happens in our lives when we are disappointed or our expectations are not meant? What if something or someone we are counting on comes up empty?

- Habakkuk says that, despite his disappointment and loss, he will still rejoice in the Lord. How is that possible? How can we give thanks to God when we are sad?

- Thomas Edison seems to say that there are no mistakes, but only opportunities for learning and growth. Can you think of examples of this in your own life?

- How do we learn not to be crushed by defeat, but instead to try again? Have you had people in your life who have taught this lesson of resilience?

- What makes "thank you" such a powerful prayer? Can you think of difficult situations where it is still possible to say "thank you"?

Tell the group:

> The hymn "It Is Well With My Soul" was written in response to one family's tragedy. Horatio Spafford wrote this hymn after the ship *Ville du Havre* sank in 1873. His wife survived, but his four daughters were drowned. While onboard another ship to join his wife in England, Spafford penned these lyrics. He describes his agony like "sorrows, like a sea billows roll." It is a frightening image of grief's ability to overtake our lives with a powerful sadness.

Sing or listen to "It Is Well With My Soul." Engage the group in conversation about the song with these questions:

REFLECTION QUESTIONS:

- What do you think made it possible for Spafford to write a hymn of praise only days after such a tragedy?
- People need time to grieve and to simply be sad. Offering a prayer of thanks should not require that our grief is forgotten or ignored. How do we find a balance between acknowledging our sorrow and trying to be aware of God's presence?

Invite the group to brainstorm a list of situations that challenge us in our daily lives. These might include (among others) death, worries about children, addiction, being a caretaker, health concerns, national/international news, and so on. Enlist a volunteer to record these responses on newsprint.

Form small groups. Ask each group to look at the list of difficult situations. Tell each group to choose one. Use the following guidelines to write a short prayer as a group. Remind the group that, as they write this prayer, they are not necessarily describing a personal experience. Rather, they are offering people and situations to God's care.

Consider these reflection questions as you write your prayer:

REFLECTION QUESTIONS:

- Name the challenging circumstances you have chosen to consider.

- Describe the emotions of someone enduring this situation.

- Discuss what might make it possible to give thanks in this situation. Could it be the kindness of friends, neighbors, or strangers? Could those in caring professions touch their lives? Might they be aware of natural beauty? What help could faith offer?

- Using these ideas, write a short prayer recognizing the painful situation and also offering thanks.

When the groups have completed the exercise, invite them to discuss the experience of writing a group prayer. Invite each group to share their prayer; these may be offered during closing worship, as well.

End the group gathering by listening "Great Is Your Faithfulness" or another song.

Crafting Our Message: Creating a Quote Box

Purpose:

Create a collection of inspirational quotes to be used as part of a gratitude practice. Participants will create a collection of quotes; they can gather additional quotes throughout the year.

The quote boxes also make a thoughtful gift; participants may choose to create a box to give away.

Materials:

- 3 x 5 inch notecards. At least a dozen per participant.

- Box to hold notecards (can be obtained at a dollar store)

- Books of inspirational quotes

- Print-outs of inspirational Scripture verses. Search the internet for Scriptures of comfort, praise, strength, or courage.

- If internet access is available, websites such as Quotes.net or Brainyquote.com offer a wide variety of quotes

- Display quotes, poems, and Scripture verses that participants have brought

- Stickers

- Pens, colored pencils, fine-tip markers

Directions:

Explain to the group that part of our gratitude practice can include feeding our spirit by reading words of wisdom, encouragement, and Scripture. This practice can be done in conjunction with writing in our gratitude journal.

Tell the group:

> Wise sayings can kickstart our personal reflection time by providing food for thought. These quotes can remind us of blessings in our lives or increase our awareness of God's presence.
>
> Everyone will create a quote box, which is a tool to encourage daily reflection and prayer. This does not have to be a time-consuming practice, but can be incorporated into routines that are already part of your lives. For example, the quote box could be kept in the kitchen, and a quote could be read every morning while waiting for coffee to brew. It could be kept by the door to access before walking the dog or kept on the table as part of grace before a meal. Put some quotes in a portable pouch to be enjoyed while waiting for a doctor's appointment or a child's sporting event.
>
> The purpose is not to create another obligation to our to-do list, but to add a meaningful moment of reflection each day.

The participants have the opportunity to make twelve to fifteen quote cards at the retreat. After the retreat, they can continue to look for quotes and Scripture verses to add to their quote box. One goal might be to make thirty-one quote cards for each day of a month, or even 365 cards for every day of the year.

Give each participant twelve to fifteen index cards. Ensure that everyone has access to pens, markers, colored pencils, and stickers.

Invite participants to look at the provided quotes and Scripture verses. Instruct the group to write one quote on each index card. They may choose to decorate the cards as well.

This process is repeated until all the cards have been filled (or time is up). The completed cards can be placed in the card holder.

Invite participants to share one of their quotes with the group. Additional quotes may be shared during closing worship.

Additional Craft Resources (for those who complete the craft early and are looking for further ideas):

- Adult coloring sheets (can be obtained free online)
- Colored pencils
- Pre-stamped postcards and pens (to be mailed by leader six to eight weeks after the retreat). Participants can write themselves a short note highlighting meaningful moments or quotes from the retreat.
- Letters of gratitude. Provide notecards, stationary, and stamps so participants may write a letter to express gratitude to someone who has touched their life.

Worship Resources:

These are themed resources for this particular retreat. Additional resources are available in the Appendix.

Litany: (Inspired by "Come, O Thankful People, Come")

> Leader: Come, you thankful people come.
>
> People: Let us lift up our voices and give thanks to God.
>
> Leader: Come, you thankful people come.
>
> People: Let us praise God our Maker, who provides for us every day.
>
> Leader: Come, you thankful people, come.
>
> People: Let us worship the God of the harvest, the God who promises to be with us always.

Litany of Thanks

(Inspired by the hymn "For The Beauty Of The Earth." These lyrics are in the public domain and may be copied.)

LEFT: When I look toward the heavens, I stand in awe of God, whose love lasts forever.

RIGHT: You, who created us and who knew us before anyone else, we thank you.

LEFT: We thank you for love that surrounds us and grace that forgives us.

RIGHT: We thank you for the beauty of your creation, which reflects your power and presence.

ALL: (singing)
For the beauty of the earth,
For the beauty of the skies,
For the love which from our birth
Over and around us lies,
Lord of all, to thee we raise
This our hymn of grateful praise

LEFT: Let us give thanks to God, for God's steadfast love endures forever. God does wondrous things.

RIGHT: God created the heavens and the earth. God made the great lights—the sun to rule over the day while the stars and moon rule over the night.

ALL (singing):
For the beauty of each hour
Of the day and of the night,
Hill and vale, and tree and flow'r,
Sun and moon, and stars of light,
Lord of all, to thee we raise
This our hymn of grateful praise

LEFT: For loving relationships, for friends that walk by our side

RIGHT: For families given to us and chosen by us

LEFT: For our congregation, united by your love

RIGHT: For the blessings of human love, we give you thanks.

ALL (singing):
For the joy of human love,
Brother, sister, parent, child,
Friends on earth, and friends above,
For all gentle thoughts and mild,
Lord of all, to thee we raise
This our hymn of grateful praise

For the good that love inspires,
For a world where none exclude,
For a faith that never tires, and for every heart renewed.
Lord of all, to thee we raise
This our hymn of grateful praise

Unison Prayers:

Giving and generous God, have we said "thank you" today? As we woke up this morning, alive and well, did we give thanks for our lives? As we gaze out of the window at the splendor of your creation, have we offered prayers of appreciation for the beauty? As we sit among friends and neighbors, have we given thanks for fellowship? We are told that if the only prayer we ever say is "thank you," that will be enough. Thank you, loving God. Thank you. Amen.

It is well with my soul.
Well, not always.
Sometimes I worry.
Often I don't sleep.
My stomach churns, my mind races.
My soul is not completely "well."

I worry about the state of the world and my to-do list keeps me up at night.
That loved one that I worry about—what will happen to her?
What about his addiction?
Will the children be all right? Are they safe?
And yet—I want it to be well with my soul. Because you promise to be with
    me.
But can you love me after what I've done? Said? Thought? Failed to do?
Does your mercy extend to vicious words I wish I could take back?
My list is long. My concerns seem un-ending.
But your love, your faithfulness—that is eternal.
More powerful than my sorrows and more lasting than my grief.
And so—it is well with my soul.
Thank you.
Amen.

Chapter 13

Advent

Preparing for a Season of Hope

About This Theme:

Advent is that brief, candle-lit season that leads us to Christmas. Society doesn't really recognize Advent; instead the world chooses to celebrate "Christmas" starting sometime around Labor Day and continuing on relentlessly until December twenty-fifth. Advent offers a vital message of hope, peace, joy, and love that can easily be lost in the noise, events, and clamor that leads us to Christmas.

Advent offers the foundation of the Christian story. Yet it is a season filled with a variety of challenges. Some people are overwhelmed by a multitude of events and family obligations. Others struggle with grief and depression as the holidays remind them of losses and loneliness. For those struggling with or recovering from addiction, the weeks between Thanksgiving and Christmas can be a time of painful endurance.

These potential obstacles are precisely why it is a compelling time to offer a retreat experience. As the leader, you will need to be sensitive to the diverse needs of participants as you explore ways to share the vitally important Advent message of hope and promise. This may be a prime opportunity to re-define what a retreat can look like. Although some people might be available for an extended time of study and renewal, many more will find a morning mini-retreat or a series of shorter "Advent get-aways" to be more realistic.

Retreat time—whether an overnight away, a Saturday morning, or a series of day or evening gatherings—can interrupt the seasonal stress and ease the crippling isolation that is too often part of holiday time. This is a chance to encourage people to slow down long enough to relish this brief, special season. In addition, Advent offers a unique opportunity to encourage participants to develop a home practice of activities such as candle lighting or Scripture reading that will enhance their Advent celebration.

A viable alternative to competing with the busy Advent season would be to offer an "Advent preparation" retreat in late October or November. This would allow participants to engage in Advent activities in preparation for the actual Advent season.

Scripture Focus:

- Isaiah 11:1–9
- Isaiah 40:1–5
- Isaiah 64:1–3
- Luke 1:8–16
- Luke 1:26–38
- Luke 2:8–14

"Quotable":

- "A little child shall lead them" (Isa 11: 6).
- "Comfort, O comfort my people" (Isa 40:1).
- "[God] has sent me to bring good news to the oppressed, to bind up the brokenhearted, to proclaim liberty to the captives, and release to the prisoners; to proclaim the year of the Lord's favor" (Isa 61:1–2).
- "They shall name him Emmanuel which means, 'God is with us'" (Matt 1:23).
- "The angel said to her, 'Do not be afraid'" (Luke 1:30).

Introductory Objects and Bring-Along Items:

Invite participants to bring an object that symbolizes Advent or Christmas for them. Some people struggle with this season, which can carry enormous emotional weight. Encourage participants to consider an object that reflects the meaning and impact that the season carries for them.

Invite participants to bring a crèche, angels, or other decorations that are meaningful to them. This can be a welcome addition to the retreat setting. During the course of the retreat, participants may wish to talk about the significance of their items.

In addition, encourage participants to bring along songs, poems, or reading that relates to this theme and which can be shared during worship or group gatherings.

Leader's Tip:

Be sure to bring along your own object that represents Advent and/or Christmas for you.

Take time to prepare some simple Advent candle holders (which may or may not be in wreath form) using real or electric candles. By using a variety of candle shapes and colors (even utilizing old or used candles) and readily available materials, you can demonstrate the accessibility of the Advent season. Advent is a church season that participants can easily celebrate at home as they count down the weeks until Christmas. Seeing these variations of Advent wreaths might encourage them to create one for themselves to remind them of the themes shared during the retreat. In addition, you may choose to include some of these ideas in the "Crafting Our Message" portion of the retreat.

Some Suggestions Include:

- Candles placed in sand in a bucket or in a foil-covered can
- Floating candles in pie pan or shallow plate
- Lumizu water-activated LED candles in a bowl of water (available online)

- Muffin tin with six cups. Place five candles in the cups, leaving the sixth cup available for greens, holly berries, beads, or other materials.

Music Resources:

Music can be interspersed throughout the retreat at mealtimes, the beginning and conclusion of group gatherings, and during worship.

During prayer or craft time, it may be soothing to have instrumental Advent or Christmas music playing in the background as you invite people to set aside the busyness of the season and enter into the spirit of waiting, hope, and expectation.

There are abundant resources for Advent music. While it can be comforting to listen solely to familiar renditions, the Good News of Advent can also be heard in arrangements or tunes that encourage participants to listen more carefully. The music listed below can be sung or simply enjoyed as a recording.

Note about Advent music: music has the power to stir up memories. The retreat leader should be aware that seasonal music can be both comforting and emotional for the listener; it would be wise to stay attuned to the reactions of the participants.

Hymns:

- "Angels We Have Heard On High" (tune: "Gloria"). Although this is a Christmas carol, this beautiful hymn echoes Advent themes of watching expectantly and wondering how God will speak to us.
- "Isaiah The Prophet Has Written Of Old" (tune: "Judas and Mary"). A wonderful way to hear the prophecies about the hope to come. Many versions include guitar chords.
- "My Heart Sings Out With Joyful Praise" (tune: "Marias Lovsang C.M.D."; alternate tune: "Ellacombe, Tallis' Third"). Mary's song, the Magnificat (Luke 1:46–55), featuring a toe-tapping Calypso beat. It may be interesting to compare the tempo, rhythm and overall feel of this song with the one listed below. How do we imagine Mary was feeling as she faced the unknown?

- "My Soul Gives Glory To My God" (tune: "Morning Song"). A song of hope echoing Mary's Magnificat (Luke 1:46–55).

Songs:

- "Dear Little Stranger" by Kate Campbell. A sweet lullaby sung to the babe in the manger.
- "Go Tell It On The Mountain" by Mahalia Jackson. This soulful rendition is filled with exuberant joy in celebration of Jesus' birth.
- "O Come, O Come Emmanuel" by Pentatonix. This lovely a cappella arrangement with beautiful harmonies enables listeners to hear this familiar hymn in a new way.
- "There Are Angels Hoverin' Round." This very singable tune is simple enough that participants could be invited to create their own verses for the group to sing.

Creating the Atmosphere—Preparing Your Retreat Space:

Creating a restful, welcoming environment can be especially important in preparation for this busy, rushed season. Display the quote posters you have created. Scatter candles, crèches, and other Advent symbols around the retreat space.

Offering a "book nook" with Advent and Christmas readings can encourage participants to enjoy some quiet moments of reflection.

Worship Area Suggestions:

When creating a worship area, these items might be included:

- Table covering for altar: fabric, scarf, or tablecloth
- Advent wreath with electric or real candles
- Crèche
- Angel(s)
- Christmas cards with beautiful images or messages

- Four small signs (made out of paper, wood, or other material), each with an Advent word: "hope," "peace," "joy," and "love" printed on it.

Activities and Discussion Questions for Group Gatherings:

These gatherings can be used in any order, depending on the needs of the group and time constraints.

Group Gathering: Celebrating Advent Words

Background:

Some common words and phrases are heard so often during Advent that their significance may be overlooked. This activity allows participants to reflect on these powerful terms.

Materials:

- Four pieces of newsprint
- Markers
- Tape
- Scripture verses printed for each participant

Activity:

Hang up a piece of newsprint with one of the four Advent words printed on it—"hope," "peace," "joy," and "love"—in each corner of the room.
Tell the group:

> The four candles of Advent often symbolize the gifts God provides: hope, peace, joy and love. We will take some time to explore the meaning of those words for us. As we listen to descriptions for each Advent word from Scripture, consider which one particularly speaks to you today. Although all the words are important, think about one that you yearn for or would like to receive from God.

Ask volunteers to read the Scriptures:

- Hope: Isaiah 40:1–5
- Peace: Romans 15:10
- Joy: Luke 2:10–14
- Love: John 3:16

Invite participants to gather by the newsprint poster with "their" word on it. The people gathered by that word will form a small group for conversation there.

Provide each group with another Scripture that corresponds with their word:

- Hope: Jeremiah 33:14–16
- Peace: Isaiah 11:1–6
- Joy: Isaiah 9:2–3, 6–7
- Love: Psalm 89:1–4

Invite one person from the group to read it out loud. Tell the small groups to engage in conversation about their chosen word with the following questions:

Discussion Questions:

- What does this word mean to you and why did you choose it today?
- What significance does this word have for you?
- If you were going to define this word, what would you say?

Following this conversation, invite each small group to record answers to the following questions on the newsprint:

- Where is this gift of God lacking today? Make a list of people or circumstances that particularly need this gift today.
- Where have you seen examples of this gift? Do you know someone who is good at sharing this gift?
- Using markers or colored pencils, create a symbol for your Advent word.

When the small groups have completed the questions, invite them to come together and share their reflections with the large group.

Group Gathering: Praying with Advent Words

Background:

Advent, this season of God coming to us, can inspire us to pray. This group gathering offers time for reflection and prayer. This activity may be done as part of worship or at a different time. There should be a place for the participants to place lighted electric votives at the conclusion of this gathering.

Materials:

- Scripture verses printed for each participant
- Reflection questions for each participant
- Votive candles for each participant

Activity:

Remind the group that the Advent candles represent God's gifts of hope, peace, joy, and love. Advent offers us the opportunity to consider who might benefit from these gifts and to lift those individuals and situations up in prayer.

Tell the group:

> We know that Christmas is the celebration of God's gift to us in Jesus. Advent provides time to think about why these gifts are needed. When we recognize our need, our gratitude for God's generosity can be increased. A gift takes on more meaning when we understand just how much that gift meets a need or fills an emptiness.

Ask four volunteers to read the Scriptures:

- Hope: Isaiah 61:1–3
- Peace: 1 Thessalonians 5:13b–24

- Joy: Luke 1:39–45

- Love: Luke 1:26–38

Provide the participants with the questions below.
Tell the group:

> We are going to take some time to consider the Advent gifts
> of hope, peace, joy, and love. You may choose to answer all of
> the questions, or you may focus on one or two of the Advent
> words and write responses to those questions.
>
> As you read over these questions, allow them to draw
> you into reflection. There is no right or wrong way to an-
> swer—this is an invitation for you to respond to God's Ad-
> vent message. Take some time to think about the gifts God
> is offering and the difference they can make in people's lives.
> As you consider the Advent words, you might think about an
> individual or group you know, people you have heard of in
> the news, or even yourself.

You may choose to play music in the background as participants spend
time with these questions. This can be a thought-provoking activity; let participants know how much time you have allotted so they will not feel rushed.

REFLECTION QUESTIONS:

Who do you know who needs the gift of hope?

- Who may be losing hope?

- Who needs encouragement?

- Who needs to be reminded that God offers new life and a fresh beginning—over and over again?

- What is your prayer for this person/these people?

Who do you know who needs the gift of peace?

- Who may feel afraid or uncertain?

- Who may feel unforgivable?

- Who can't quiet their mind or spirit?

- Who is perhaps harder on themselves than necessary?
- What is your prayer for this person/these people?

Who do you know who needs the gift of joy?

- Who hasn't laughed in a long time?
- Who is carrying a heavy burden?
- Who seems weary in spirit?
- Whose life would you like to be interrupted by God's abounding love?
- What is your prayer for this person/these people?

Who do you know who needs the gift of love?

- Who has forgotten that s/he is a beloved child of God?
- Who has been told lies about themselves or their value?
- Who may think they are unloved or unlovable?
- What is your prayer for this person/these people?

As participants complete their reflections, bring the group back together. Invite the participants to share any reactions or reflections from this exercise.

When everyone has had an opportunity to speak, tell the group:

> Everyone is invited to think of someone who needs God's gifts. You are invited to light a votive candle and place it on the altar. You can say that person's name silently or out loud.

The group gathering can close by listening to "O Come, O Come Emmanuel" or another song.

Group Gathering: Message for You

Background:

Angels bring messages from God. Participants will create an Advent message to take home to remind them of Advent's good news of hope.

Materials:

- Christmas cards (these can just be the "faces" of the card without the inside message)
- Construction paper in a variety of colors
- Scissors
- Glue
- Markers
- Scriptures to read out loud
- "Quotable" passages on newsprint

Activity:

Tell the group that the word "angel" means "messenger." God's angels bring (sometimes surprising) messages of hope and encouragement, reminding us that God is always with us. Advent is a season when we are invited to be especially aware of the many ways God is speaking to us.

Invite the group to listen to angel voices in the Scriptures listed below. Encourage them to be especially attentive to the recurring message of "Do not be afraid."

Ask volunteers to read these passages about angels, one at a time:

- Angel speaks to Zechariah: Luke 1:8–15
- Angel speaks to Mary: Luke 1:26–33
- Angel speaks to Joseph: Matthew 1:18–21
- Angel speaks to the shepherds: Luke 2:8–14

Invite the group to wonder how God speaks to us today. Ask if they have any examples of experiences when they sensed God sending them a message of reassurance, comfort, or love. These do not need to be dramatic, "earth-shattering" revelations, but may be examples of any time a message was received through another person, nature, or other circumstances.

Tell the group they have the opportunity to create a message to take home. Since God is still speaking to God's people, we can consider what message God might have for us today.

Invite the group to look at the Christmas cards and to select one or two that appeal to them. Encourage them to look at the Scripture quotes that you have hung up or provided in the retreat booklet. Tell them they will use the Christmas cards to create a personalized mini-poster that provides a message to remind them of the promise of Advent and Christmas. Invite them to glue their chosen card(s) onto construction paper, and to write a Scripture quote or other phrase on the paper.

When everyone has created an Advent message, invite participants to talk about what the card image and quote means to them.

Group Gathering: Part of the Story

Background:

By identifying with one of the crèche figures, participants can immerse themselves into the Christmas story.

Materials:

- Crèche figures
- Reflection questions for each participant
- Pens

Activity:

Invite the group to gather so that everyone can see the crèche(s). Invite them to name the characters that they see who are all part of the Christmas story. This should include:

- Mary
- Joseph
- Jesus
- Angel
- Shepherds
- Stable animals

- Wise ones/magi

  - A star may not be part of the crèche set, but a symbolic star or light could be placed by the manger scene

Invite the participants to consider all of these characters and to focus on one that they are intrigued by or drawn to or interested in. Give them a few moments to choose which figure they want to focus on.

Provide them with the following questions:

REFLECTION QUESTIONS:

- What characteristics do you imagine this figure to have?
- Why do you think God chose this figure to be part of the first Christmas?
- What questions would you like to ask this figure?
- What can this figure teach you about your life or situation?

When the participants have had an opportunity to answer these questions on their own, they can share in two ways. Depending on the size of the group, participants can gather with others who chose the same figure, or gather two or three figures together (i.e., Joseph, sheep, star; Mary, shepherds, Magi).

Place the figures in different areas of the room and ask the participants to sit where they find their chosen figure so they can discuss the questions together.

Group Gathering: Why Do We Need Advent?

Background:

The season of Advent begins by people realizing that they need God's help. Christmas is the celebration of Christ's birth. Advent provides us with the time to ponder why we need God to come to us and why we need God's transforming love.

Materials:

- Copy of Isaiah 64:1–3
- Song: "Isaiah The Prophet Has Written Of Old"
- Newsprint
- Sticky notes, five or six for each participant
- Markers
- Pens

Activity:

Let the group know that, before Jesus was born, the prophets foretold his birth in the Hebrew Scriptures. They cried out to God, asking for a savior to transform their desperate situation. Isaiah speaks to God forcefully and almost demands that God do something. Isaiah is convinced that the world is in a terrible state which will not change without God's intervention.

Invite the group to listen for Isaiah's words in the song "Isaiah The Prophet Has Written Of Old."

Ask for a volunteer to read Isaiah 64:1–3 out loud. Instruct the group to listen for Isaiah's strong words—he wants God to do something! Isaiah is describing a situation of despair and need to God. Isaiah wants God to respond to these desperate circumstances and bring order into this chaos.

With this in mind, tell participants to listen to Isaiah's plea as another volunteer reads Isaiah 64:1–3 once more.

Provide each participant with five or six sticky notes and a pen or marker. Tell participants to write down answers to these questions:

- What situations need God's help?
- Where do we want God to act?

Invite them to be specific and use the sticky notes to record the names of people or situations where God's help is needed. When they are done writing, invite them to stick the notes on sheets of newsprint.

Invite the participants to engage with these responses:

- Read all the responses out loud.

- Invite the group to listen to the responses and to notice if there are similarities between them.

- Ask the group to come up with some broad categories that fit these responses. These categories are reasons why we need God's presence. Some examples might be "prayers for others," "prayers for self," "prayers for country," and so on. Some responses may not fit neatly into any one category; these can be listed as "other reasons."

- Write these categories individually at the top of sheets of newsprints. Move the individual sticky notes to the category where they best fit. This will give a visual impression of the reasons why we are (like Isaiah) asking God to act in our lives.

- Review the lists of reasons. Ask the group if there is anything they would like to add to the list, or if there is anything on the list that surprises them.

Invite the participants to choose one of the categories. Form small groups based on the chosen category, and use the words and phrases listed on the sticky notes to write a short prayer. Tell each small group:

> You are invited to be like Isaiah and state your plea to God. Write an Advent prayer asking for God's help.

These prayers can be used in closing worship, if desired.

Crafting Our Message: Interactive Advent Calendar

Purpose:

To create an intentional, interactive Advent calendar which encourages meaningful Advent activities.

Materials:

- Newsprint
- Markers
- Colored pencils
- Advent or Christmas stickers

- Advent and Christmas-themed stamps and stamp pads
  - List of Advent Scriptures for each participant
  - Pre-printed calendar page with the four weeks of Advent for each participant. This should be sturdy enough to use every day. For example, the calendar can be printed on an 8 x 11 inch piece of paper and then mounted onto card stock. Leave a margin around the edges of the calendar to encourage decoration and personalization.

Directions:

Tell the participants they are each going to create an Advent calendar that will reinforce the theme of the message of Advent. We will be discovering ways to listen for that message, as well as to be messengers of hope ourselves. The participants will have the chance to personalize their Advent calendar with Scriptures and simple activities that reinforce the Advent message of hope.

Divide the participants into small groups (four to five people) and encourage them to think creatively about how both to receive and give the message of Advent joy and hope. What will help them hold onto Advent during this busy season? What could help them share the spirit of hope, peace, joy, and love with others?

Some suggestions might include:

- Pay it forward at a drive-through window
- Read a poem
- Look at the stars. Really look and be amazed.
- Smile at someone on the street or in line with you
- Read a children's book about Jesus' birth
- Sit down and listen to a favorite Christmas song. Breathe deeply, then listen again.

Ask the small groups to brainstorm ideas and record as many as possible on a piece of newsprint.

When the groups have written down several ideas, ask them to hang up the newsprint so it is visible to the entire group. Briefly invite each small group to read their ideas and provide any additional explanation. Ideally, the group will collectively present more than twenty-eight ideas so that participants will have an abundance to choose from.

Give each participant a blank Advent calendar and a list of Advent Scriptures. Explain that they are invited to create a calendar that help them celebrate Advent. They can personalize their own calendar by choosing from among the activities and readings.

These are some of the options available to them:

- Record a different Scripture for every day

- Record one Scripture for the week and read that passage every day

- Choose the activities that are most appealing. Any activities (or readings) may be repeated.

Advent Scriptures (these could also be listed on a bookmark for easy reference):

- Isaiah 9:2–7
- Isaiah 11:1–10
- Isaiah 40:1–5
- Isaiah 60:1–6
- Isaiah 61:1–4
- Isaiah 61:8–11
- Isaiah 64:1–3
- Jeremiah 33:14–16
- Micah 5:2–5
- Psalm 80:1–7
- 1 Thessalonians 5:14–24
- Luke 1:5–10
- Luke 1:11–17
- Luke 1:18–25

- Luke 1:26–38
- Luke 1:39–45
- Luke 1:46–56
- Luke 2:1–5
- Luke 2:6–7
- Luke 2:8–12
- Luke 2:13–14
- Luke 2:15–18
- Luke 2:19–20
- Matthew 2:1–2
- Matthew 2:3–6
- Matthew 2:7–8
- Matthew 2:9–12
- John 1:1–5

Additional Craft Resources (for those who complete the craft early and are looking for further ideas):

- Adult coloring sheets (can be obtained free online)
- Colored pencils
- Pre-stamped postcards and pens (to be mailed by leader six to eight weeks after the retreat). Participants can write themselves a short note highlighting meaningful moments or quotes from the retreat.

Worship Resources:

These are themed resources to go with this particular retreat. Additional resources are available in the Appendix.

Litanies:

Leader: It is Advent and there are angels hovering 'round.

People: They remind us that God hears us in our need.

Leader: We look for signs and miracles, we pray for God to be Emmanuel, always with us.

People: It is Advent. We listen, we wait, we search, and we hope.

Leader: Arise, shine, for your light is come.

People: Faithful God, we thank you for sending light into our darkness.

Leader: Arise, shine, for your light is come.

People: Generous God, we thank you for giving us the precious gift of your Son, Jesus.

Leader: Arise, shine, for your light is come.

People: We offer ourselves to you so that your light may shine through us.

Leader: If we watch, we can receive the announcement of the angel.

People: "Do not be afraid, for see—I am bringing you good news of great joy for all people."

Leader: If we look, we can see a miracle in our midst.

People: "You will find a child lying in a manger."

Leader: If we listen, we hear the sound of the angels' song.

People: "Glory to God in the highest heaven and on earth peace among all people."

Leader: With Mary's greeting, Elizabeth's child leaped for joy.

People: May we be reminded that God's voice speaks to our spirits to offer us hope, peace, joy, and love.

Leader: Mary gave thanks for God's gift saying, "My soul magnifies the Lord and my spirit rejoices in God my Savior."

People: Even in the midst of fear and unrest, may our souls rejoice in the faithfulness of God.

Leader: Mary was humbled that God looked with favor upon her.

People: We too are entrusted with God's Good News. May we also be faithful messengers, sharing God's presence.

Unison Prayers

God of light, you announce that you break through the darkness of our despair every day. How is it that we miss you? Is your light so bright that we are blinded by your presence? Or are we looking in the wrong direction? During this season of watching and waiting, remind us to go where you are—to the lost, the lonely and the broken-hearted. Help us to recognize your Good News that you choose to dwell among us. Wonderful Counselor, we thank you. Amen.

Lord, we have long lists of things yet to do. Will we make time to invite you into our lives? Our ears are filled with endless loops of Christmas music. Will we hear you remind us to "be not afraid" and your assurance that "The Lord is with you"? We have lists, we have worries, we have stress. Is there room in our lives for the miracles around us? Our minds dwell on plans and details. Will we take a moment to "ponder your words in our hearts"? As Advent slips away and Christmas approaches, help us be aware that you are Emmanuel, always with us. And let us celebrate that in our hearts and in our deeds. Amen.

Appendix 1

Additional Worship Resources

EACH RETREAT INCLUDES WORSHIP materials that coordinate with the particular theme. These additional materials can be used in any of the retreats.

Litanies

Leader: Whether we are strangers or old friends, in this place, God is joining us together as one.

People: Whether we are young or old, the Spirit is building bridges to bring us together as one.

Leader: We come together to be made whole. We come together to build a bridge.

People: A bridge of light! A bridge of strength! A bridge of justice! A bridge of love!

Leader: Whatever barriers we try to put between us, barriers of generation, experience or culture, God removes them to build a strong bridge between all of God's people.

People: We are ready to use all that God has given us to bring hope and healing and life to our world so we may live together as God's people.

Leader: Welcoming God, you invite us to come to you with all that is on our hearts and minds.

People: You encourage us to pray every day, in every way we know how, for everyone we know.

Leader: You welcome our pleas for help and strength, as well as our words of praise and thanksgiving.

People: We offer you our prayers and intercessions, grateful that you care about the concerns on our hearts.

Litanies Inspired by Scripture

Genesis 8

Leader: We come together to worship our Creator.

People: We give thanks for the beauty of the earth and all of its creatures.

Leader: We come together to worship God, who calls us to care for creation.

People: We offer our hands, our hearts and ourselves so we may share God's compassion for everything and everyone on earth.

Leader: We come together in awe of the strength of the storm, the power of the wind, the destructive force of the water.

People: We come as the created to worship our Creator.

Deuteronomy 6

Leader: Hear, O Israel, the Lord is our God, the Lord alone.

People: It is God we are meant to serve and God whom we must please. No one else.

Leader: You shall love the Lord your God with all your heart, all your soul, and all your might.

People: Our words and our actions should reflect our love for God.

1 Samuel 3 and John 1:43–51

Leader: God surprised Samuel by calling him in the middle of the night.

People: Samuel replied, "Speak, Lord, for your servant listens." This was the beginning of a lifetime of faithfulness.

Leader: Jesus invited his disciples into service by calling them and saying, "Follow me."

People: Their hearts responded with joy because they knew that some deep need within them was being answered.

Leader: Philip said to Nathanael, "This is one whom we have been seeking." When Nathanael was doubtful, Philip simply said, "Come and see."

People: This is evangelism—inviting someone to experience the good news of Jesus Christ. May we be willing to share the love and mercy that is given to us.

1 Corinthians 12

Leader: For the mosaics of our lives, patterns of people and experiences that enrich us, we give you thanks.

People: For bringing all these different people, opinions, and backgrounds together to form your church, we thank you.

Leader: For calling us the Body of Christ, consisting of endless varieties of gifts and talents, we give you thanks.

People: Creator and creative God, open us to your spirit and bring us together to form a vision of your new life and hope.

1 Corinthians 15

Leader: Over the noise and confusion of our lives, Jesus calls us to come and follow.

People: We are called to focus on the mystery of our faith—that Jesus lived, Jesus died, and Jesus rose again.

Leader: Over the tumult, in the midst of chaos, Jesus calls us to share peace and hope.

People: We are called to speak of God's love and to share God's message of new life.

Unison Prayers

Generous God, throughout the Epiphany season we celebrate your gifts of light and renewal. Ignite the fire of your love within so that we may answer your call to be the messengers of your story. As we share the good news of your Son, Jesus, help us to pass on your gospel of forgiveness and love through our actions and our words. In Jesus' name we pray. Amen.

Faithful God, Creator of the universe, thank you for your abundant blessings. Let our gratitude be seen in our love for you. Forgive us when we try to impress you or each other. Remind us that your forgiveness and grace are your loving gifts to us, freely given. We cannot earn your love. Instead, we come and acknowledge that we need your gift of new life. Help us offer our gratitude and praise through lives filled with service of you and your children, near and far. Amen.

Here we are, Lord, standing in the need of prayer. We pray for our brothers and sisters and also for ourselves, that we may know your will and follow in your way. Thank you inviting us to lay our burdens down and entrust our cares to you. Forgive us when we think we have to shoulder every problem alone and struggle on through life without help. Remind us that you journey with us and guide us like a good shepherd. As you care and nurture us, help us to offer care and comfort to your children all around us. In Jesus' name we pray. Amen.

Holy One, you made the Earth and all that is in it. We give thanks for the sky and the seas, the mountains and the valleys, the trees and the flowers, the birds that fly and the fish that swim and all the animals that walk or crawl or creep on the land. You called on human beings to care for creation, to serve you and praise you by loving all you have made. We don't always do it well.

Forgive us for the ways we fail to love your world and your people with our whole hearts. Open our eyes to recognize the need around us and help us to respond with willing hands and loving hearts. Amen.

Living God, you speak words of love and truth. Your voice is filled with grace and forgiveness. Your word is alive and fills us with hope. We are humbled that you give us the privilege of free will and entrust us to share your vision of unity and justice. When our words do not reflect your living Word of new life, forgive us. We can choose to offer one another encouragement and support, or we can speak impatient words of bitterness and scorn. Remind us of the power of our voice. Let our hearts, our actions, and our voices reflect the transforming power of your love. Amen.

God of yesterday, today, and forever, thank you for your faithfulness. No matter how the world changes, your steadfast love endures forever. Help us remember that you always offer forgiveness and new life. Forgive us when we are grudging in our response to you. When we withhold our hearts or hesitate to love with our minds and spirits, have mercy on us. Help us to dare serve you by working for justice and sharing your life-changing kindness. Amen.

Deuteronomy 6:4–9

"Hear, O Israel: The Lord is our God, the Lord alone. You shall love the Lord your God with all your heart, and all your soul, and with all your might. Keep these words that I am commanding you today in your heart. Recite them to your children and talk about them when you are at home and when you are away, when you lie down and when you rise. Bind them as a sign on your hand, fix them as an emblem on your forehead, and write them on the doorposts of your house and on your gate."

1 Thessalonians 1:1–10

Giving and generous God, have we said "thank you" today? As we woke up this morning, alive and well, did we give thanks for our lives? As we gaze out of the window at the splendor of your creation, have we told you that we appreciate the beauty? As we sit among friends and neighbors, have we given thanks for fellowship? Meister Eckhart told us that if the only prayer we ever say is "thank you," that will be enough. Thank you, loving God. Thank you. Amen

Appendix 2

Additional Music Resources

IN ADDITION TO THE songs and hymns listed in each chapter, these resources provide a wide-ranging variety of musical options.

Songs:

- "Dear Hate" by Maren Morris and Vince Gill. Released after the 2017 Las Vegas shooting, this song informs Hate that Love will conquer all. This encouraging song acknowledges pain while lifting up the power of love.

- "Draw The Circle Wide" by Mark Miller. An excellent way to begin or end any retreat, this song celebrates God's welcoming circle of love.

- "Dream God's Dream" by Bryan Sirchio. This uplifting song echoes themes from the "I have a dream" speech by Martin Luther King Jr., and encourages listeners to share God's light.

- "Farewell, Good Friends" (Tune: Shalom). A simple blessing with both English and Hebrew text which can be sung as a round. A nice way to end a retreat.

- "Go Safely Into The Night" by the Ennis Sisters. This lullaby-like song can be used as a lovely prayer and benediction; it offers an excellent way to end an evening program as participants "go safely into the night."

- "Grace Like Rain" by Todd Agnew. A new twist to the beloved hymn "Amazing Grace."

- "Shall We Gather: Hymns & Inspiring Airs" by Kim Robertson. Played on the Celtic harp, this album contains a series of beautiful hymns. A wonderful collection for worship, craft, or meditation time.

- "Songs Of Grace: New Hymns For God And Neighbor" by Carolyn Winfrey Gillette (Nashville: Discipleship, 2009). New, compelling lyrics set to familiar hymn tunes. Permission is granted to use the texts in public worship when acknowledgement of the author and source is provided. This is a valuable tool for anyone searching for relevant themes to share in worship.

Songs for Communion:

If you choose to celebrate communion, these lovely songs can help participants reflect on the Lord's table.

- "Come To The Table Of Grace" (Tune: Table of Grace). This lovely hymn has a simple tune and is easily learned without the need of providing printed lyrics.

- "For Everyone Born" (Tune: For Everyone Born). Shirley Erena Murray's welcoming and inclusive hymn (written in 1998) has been updated with a verse specifically naming the LGBT community as having "a place at the table."

- "The Last Song" by Kate Campbell. An evocative imagining of Jesus gathering with his disciples for his last supper and a shared last song.

- "Table Of Friendship And Love" by Bryan Sirchio. Almost everyone can remember the awkwardness of the high school cafeteria. Bryan Sirchio reimagines it as a place of welcome and acceptance.

Additional Song Suggestions:

Chapter 2: Following the Star: Celebrating Epiphany Together

- "Window in the Skies": U2

Chapter 3: Self Care: Tending to Our Spirit

- "Bridge Over Troubled Waters": Simon and Garfunkel
- "Help": The Beatles
- "Here Comes The Sun": The Beatles

Chapter 4: Discovering Our Voices: Exploring the Adventures of Ruth

- "Could You Be": Peter Mayer

Chapter 5: Hope and Transformation: Discovering the Hidden Potential in Everyone

- "Beautiful Day": U2
- "One Love": Bob Marley
- "People Get Ready": The Impressions

Chapter 7: Roots and Branches: Reflecting on Our Past, Preparing for Our Future

- "New Year's Day," "Zoo Station": U2
- "Church Of The Earth": Peter Mayer
- "In My Life": The Beatles

Chapter 8: Teach Us to Pray: Discovering Creative Spirituality

- "Bountiful": Peter Mayer
- "Let It Be": The Beatles

Chapter 9: Created in God's Image: Affirming Ourselves and Welcoming Others

- "Everyday People": Sly and the Family Stone

Chapter 10: Wherever You Go: Celebrating Special Relationships

- "All You Need Is Love": The Beatles
- "Lean On Me": Bill Withers
- "Stand By Me": Ben E. King
- "We Are Going To Be Friends": White Stripes
- "With A Little Help From My Friends": The Beatles

Chapter 11: Experiencing Wilderness: Friends on the Journey through Challenging Times

- "Blackbird": The Beatles
- "Exodus": Bob Marley
- "Get Up, Stand Up": Bob Marley
- "The Longest Night": Peter Mayer

Chapter 12: Practicing Daily Gratitude: Developing Awareness of God's Blessings

- "Blue Skies": Ella Fitzgerald
- "Bountiful": Peter Mayer
- "People Get Ready": Impressions
- "Thankful N' Thoughtful": Sly & the Family Stone

Appendix 3

Questions of the Day

DISPLAY TWO TO THREE questions and encourage participants to thoughtfully consider and offer anonymous responses. Be sure to provide markers! Invite them to discuss the questions during meals or free time. If you choose, answers can be read aloud at the closing of the retreat.

Some Sample Questions (Feel Free to Add Your Own!):

- What surprised you most this week?
- Today I just want to . . .
- What movie quote describes your past, present, or future . . .?
- What is the kindest thing someone has done for you lately?
- If you could go anywhere in the world right now, where would you go?
- What advice would you give your younger self?
- What lesson have you learned this year?
- What good news have you received lately?
- List two or three adjectives that describe what you believe about yourself.
- What do you wish people could know about you by just looking?
- What song describes your mood right now?
- If you could do anything without worrying about judgment, what would you do?

Appendix 4

Icebreakers

Or, Getting the Conversation Started

PEOPLE JOIN GROUPS OR go on retreats because they want to spend time with others and perhaps learn from each other. When members in a group do not know each other, it can sometimes be challenging to get a conversation started. This is even more important when some are acquainted but others are new to the group. These simple exercises offer non-threatening ways to remove some barriers and build trust and community. They are an excellent way to set a relaxed atmosphere and encourage laughter and sharing.

Icebreakers offer participants the opportunity to break the ice with one another. If members of your group need to learn one another's names, these games and exercises can help. Even if everyone is already acquainted, these exercises invite people to get to know one another in a more informal, light-hearted manner, which will lead to a deeper level as time progresses. Many church groups discover that Sunday mornings do not always offer a chance to get beyond a polite "good morning" with very little follow-up conversation. These simple exercises offer a bit more depth without threatening introverts in the group with over-sharing. Even groups who are well-acquainted will often discover some unknown tidbit about the other participants; this helps strengthen the bond that is formed during a retreat experience.

The icebreakers generate brief answers and short conversations that lay the groundwork for important sharing.

Each exercise takes only a few minutes, so more than one can be used at any one time. The exercises can be used at different times throughout the retreat; for example, as an alternative to the music or poetry suggestions when the large group reconvenes, in preparation for the next large group activity.

Name/Letter Association

Sometimes the best name games are the easiest ones. This simple exercise offers participants the opportunity to remember each other's names by using a simple mnemonic device.

Materials: N/A

How to Play:

- Invite the group to gather in a circle, seated or standing.
- Go around the circle and invite each person to say their name and to list an object or an adjective that starts with the same letter as their name. For example, "My name is Sue and I am stunning." Or they can name a favorite food; "I am Sue and my favorite food is soup."
- If you would like to tie the object or adjective into the theme, that is an option. But this is meant to be a fun exercise, so encourage people to say whatever comes to mind. If there are many people whose names begin with the same letter (think Jill, Jessica, Jane, and Joy), it can be a challenge. The individual is welcome to turn to the group for suggestions.
- Once everyone has had a turn, the leader can go around the circle quickly and name each person and "their" corresponding word.
- Very often participants will remember the adjective first and that will help them recall the person's name.

"Speed Chat" or "Round Robin"

This activity offers participants the chance for quick, light conversations with a number of people.

Materials:

- Chairs, one for each person (optional)
- List of questions for the leader

How to Play:

- This exercise can be done seated or standing, depending on your group. I have found that having people seated encourages a longer conversation.
- Arrange half the chairs in a circle facing out, away from one another. Arrange the second half of chairs to face this first set. The two circles are facing one another. The chairs are in pairs so that one person is on the inner circle facing one person in the outer circle. If there are an odd number of participants, the leader can join in to make the number even.

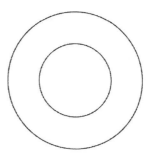

- Invite those who might have mobility concerns or who would simply rather remain seated throughout the entire exercise to sit in the inner circle of chairs. The people in the outer circle of chairs will be moving often.
- Once everyone has found a chair, explain that you will read a question. They will talk with the person seated opposite them. When the leader senses that conversation is lagging (or when the leader wishes to move the participants along), the leader will ring a bell. The inner circle of people remains seated. The outer circle of people all move to the next chair on their right. Now everyone is facing a different conversation partner.

- The leader asks a new question and invites participants to talk with their new conversation partner. Continue asking questions until the participants return to their original conversation partner.

Speed-Chat Questions:

These can be customized to coordinate with the theme of the retreat, if desired. If, however, the purpose is simply to encourage people to begin to get to know one another, these questions work well.

- Where did you live when you were ten years old? Who did you live with?
- Can you name all the places you have lived?
- Have you had a favorite pet in your lifetime?
- Have you ever climbed a tree? Where was it?
- If you could choose any view to see out of your window, what would it be?
- Do you have a favorite flower? What is it?
- Do you have a garden? What grows in it?
- What do you like to do in your free time?
- When you are upset, name something that helps you calm down.
- Were you part of a special group as a child—a church, scouts, a team, or club?
- What did your room look like when you were a teenager? What was on the walls? What color was it? Did you share a room?
- What kind of work do you do/have you done?
- If you could try any kind of work, what would it be?
- What was something fun you did in the last week?
- How did you picture God as a child?
- How do you picture God now, if at all?
- Who is a famous person you'd like to meet?
- Name one to two things on your bucket list.
- What's your favorite food for supper? Breakfast?

- What is comfort food for you?
- What was your first job?

Beanbag Toss Name Game

This exercise is popular with all ages—I have played it with students as young as eight and retreatants as "old" as eighty-five. There is often a lot of laughing that goes along with this, which is an excellent icebreaker all by itself.

Remind the participants that the goal is not necessarily to be successful, but rather to have a chance to hear everyone's name and enjoy the process of remembering them.

Materials:

- Five to eight beanbags, beanbag animals, or small Nerf balls

How to Play:

- Invite the group to stand in a tight circle, shoulder to shoulder.
- Invite them to introduce themselves to the person on their right and left. Then ask the participants to say their name, one at a time, around the circle. This can be quite quick—just rapid-fire, one name after the other.
- Ask everyone to stand with their hands visible in front of them.
- Explain the process:
- The leader will go first. Take a beanbag, call out the name of someone standing opposite you. Once you are sure you have that person's attention, toss the beanbag to him/her.
- The action continues in the same manner. The person who caught the beanbag chooses someone to throw to. S/he must first call out that person's name, then throw the beanbag.
- Once a person has caught and thrown the beanbag, they put their hands down or behind them to indicate that they have already had a turn.

- The action continues until everyone has caught and thrown the beanbag. The last person will throw the beanbag back to you (or whoever had it first and was the first one to throw).

- Review: Make sure everyone remembers who they threw to! This is important—the throwing pattern will remain the same, and players will always throw to the same person.

- Begin the action again; throw the beanbag to the person you originally tossed the beanbag to.

- When four or five people have had a turn, the leader introduces a second beanbag, throwing it to the same person.

- Repeat with as many beanbags as you dare! We have had seven or eight beanbags flying (gently) around at a time, causing much laughter.

- When the pattern has been repeated three or four times, you can start "retiring" the beanbags one at a time as they arrive back to you.

- During the final round, everyone will hear the individual names being called out again.

- When the final beanbag has been caught by you, invite the group to give themselves a round of applause for a job well done!

Roll the Dice!

This works best in small groups (five to six people). This is a fun way to learn something about each other—but everyone does not necessarily address the same topic. It all depends on the roll of the dice!

Materials:

- A pair of dice per group.
- Set of eleven questions.

How to Play:

- Sit in a circle so everyone can see and hear one another. Invite the first person to roll the dice, read the corresponding question out loud and answer that question. The next person rolls the dice, answers the question, and so on.

- Alternatively, one person can roll the dice and everyone in the group can answer that particular question. This can take place whenever new small groups are formed as a conversation-starter.

Questions:

2. If you could do any job in the world for one day, what would it be?

3. What historical figure would you like to invite for dinner?

4. What is your favorite holiday? Why?

5. What would be the ideal contents in a picnic basket?

6. You suddenly have a free day without any obligations. What will you do?

7. If you could rid the world of one thing, what would it be?

8. What is something you have that is of sentimental value?

9. What would you rather have: A chauffer, a cook, or a maid? Why?

10. What's your favorite room in your house and why?

11. What's a favorite place you've travelled (or someplace you'd like to travel)?

12. What is something that frightens you?

Pieces of the Puzzle

There are many variations to this exercise. It can be a way to get people talking, it can introduce some themes of the retreat, and it can be used as a way to divide the large group into smaller groups. It is a way to do some group problem-solving and encourage people to work together.

Materials:

- You can use a very simple (six-to-eight piece) children's puzzle (available online or at baby stores).
- You can make your own puzzles on card stock (8.5 x 11 or 8.5 x 14 inches).
- The image might be a Scripture passage, quote, or picture that coordinates with the theme.
- Google Images is a good resource for quotes and pictures.

How to Play:

- Depending on the size of your group, you should have three to five puzzles, with enough puzzle pieces that everyone can have one piece.
- Give everyone a piece of a puzzle. Tell them how many puzzles there are in total and let them know that their challenge is to put all the puzzles together by finding the matching parts.
- Invite the participants to find the coordinating pieces so they can complete the image on their puzzle together on a table.
- When they have put the puzzle together, invite each group to introduce each other.
- The activity by itself gets people talking with one another as they compare puzzle pieces and try to find the correct matches. Once the puzzle has been fit together, those people can now form a small group for conversation, if desired.
- This activity can be repeated every time you want to create new groupings.

One Group, Many Variations

This exercise gets people talking and moving around. As an additional challenge, the leader could invite participants to do one round without talking.

Materials:

- List of direction statements for leader

How to Play:

- Tell participants you would like them to form a line. The order of the line will depend on the criteria listed. Optional: creating a line on the floor with tape will help them get back in line when the criteria changes.
- Variation 1: Line up by birth month, January—December
- Variation 2: Line up according to birthplace—farthest to closest
- Variation 3: Line up alphabetically by first name, A–Z
- Variation 4: Line up according to how many siblings you have, from least to most

Group Bingo

This game allows people to ask one another simple questions as they get to know one another. The leader will determine what will qualify as a "bingo" (all the spaces filled, the four corners, straight line, or diagonal).

Materials:

- Bingo sheet for each person (create a free bingo template at myfree-bingocards.com)
- Pen or pencil for each person

How to Play:

- Each participant receives a bingo sheet and a pen or pencil
- Invite participants to find a person who can answer "yes" to the description listed

- Write down that person's name
- Now move on to another person. The goal is to talk with as many people as possible. One person should not appear in two spaces.
- The game ends when someone fills in all the squares or achieves the "bingo" described by the leader

Bingo Questions: Find a Person Who

- Likes to garden
- Rides a bicycle
- Has pets (what kind?)
- Speaks a second language
- Has experienced a tornado or earthquake
- Likes to wash dishes
- Has participated in a marathon
- Knows how to make a pie crust
- Has traveled outside this country
- Likes their middle name (what is it?)
- Has lived in another state (where?)
- Has met a celebrity (who?)
- Can name the first five books of the Bible
- Can list at least five of the commandments
- Has been to Walt Disney World/Disneyland
- Has ridden on a motorcycle
- Has a tattoo
- Knows how to knit
- Has ever played an instrument
- Can name at least five planets

Pass the Hat! Introductory Questions

This is designed to be a fun, quick way to offer some initial introductions and an invitation for people to share briefly on a wide variety of topics.

There are two ways to use these introductory questions.

Option 1:

Materials:

- Enough slips of paper with one printed question for each participant
- A bell, whistle, or other noisemaker
- A hat

How to Play:

Pass the hat and invite everyone to take a slip of paper. Instruct all the participants to take their question and to engage as many people with that question as possible. Remind them to ask each other's name if they don't know. Each person will ask the question listed on their slip of paper and then have the opportunity to answer the other person's question.

After approximately sixty seconds, use the bell or whistle to indicate that it is time to find another conversation partner. Depending on the size of your group, this can be done several times.

Option 2:

Materials:

- Enough slips of paper with one printed question for each participant
- A hat

How to Play:

Invite the participants to form a seated circle. Pass the hat to the first person and instruct them to choose a slip of paper. Invite them to briefly answer the question.

Continue to pass the hat until everyone has had a turn.

With both options, encourage the group to listen for questions they find particularly interesting or engaging. Encourage them to ask these questions of one another during the remainder of the retreat during breaks or mealtimes.

Questions:

- If money were no object, what kind of car would you drive?
- How many pets have you had, if any?
- On a scale of one to ten, with ten being the best, how much fun is a flea market?
- If you were elected president, what is the first law you would pass?
- If there could only be one flavor of ice cream, what would you like it to be?
- How long could you go without a cell phone?
- If you could be an animal, what would it be?
- What is your favorite portion of a worship service?
- Can you name any of the books of the Bible?
- Who is someone who taught you about faith?
- How many places have you lived since you were born?
- What are your favorite and least favorite vegetables?
- What is your most memorable movie of all time?
- What was your favorite TV show as a child?
- If you could choose which decade of your life to repeat, which would it be?
- Don't give a name, but do you have a friend or relative you would rather not invite to an upscale event at your home? Why?

- Did you ever go to a wrestling match? If not, would you want to?
- Which would you choose for a week on a desert island—a book or a case of something good to drink?
- Who would you choose to play you in a biography of your life?
- For one million dollars, would you walk on a nude beach in the prevailing attire? If not, how much would it take?
- What's one thing on your bucket list?
- What is one place you've always wanted to visit?
- What is a place you have visited that you would like to return to?
- What's your favorite season and why?
- Do you think blondes really have more fun?
- Who was your favorite teacher? Why?
- What was your first day of high school like?
- Did you like high school? Why or why not?
- Was there someone you envied when you were young who turned out to be a disappointment? No names please.
- Did you ever get caught smoking at a young age?
- Did you know all your grandparents?
- Do you remember anything about your neighbors growing up?
- Are there any police officers in your family? Firefighters? Military? Magicians?
- Are there any clowns or circus performers in your family? Cowboys? Politicians?
- What did you want to be when you grew up?
- How many states have you traveled to/through?
- Have you traveled outside the country? Where?
- What's one of the nicest vacations you've ever had?
- When someone says "Boston" (or choose another city) what do you think of?
- What is your favorite tree?
- What is your favorite flower?

- Did you ever get a traffic ticket?
- What is something (you are willing to share) that people don't know about you?
- Have you ever worked on a night shift? If so, did you like it?
- Have you ever watched the sun rise or set? Where is/was your favorite spot to watch this happen?
- Do you or did you ever play an instrument?
- If money were no object, what would be your dream way to spend a whole day?

Made in the USA
Middletown, DE
27 April 2023

29541537R00157